CONTENTS

Glossary and Abbreviations		2
Acknowledgements		2
Addenda/Errata to Volumes 1 and 2		3
Chapter 1	Iran's Last Chance	4
Chapter 2	Two Armies	29
Chapter 3	Saddam's First Blow	43
Chapter 4	Iranian Burn-Out	55
Chapter 5	End Game	66
Camouflage and Markings		74
Bibliography		79

List of maps
Map 1	The Fish Lake Line.	6
Map 2	Operations Karbala-4 and Karbala-5.	12
Map 3	The Iraqi liberation of the Faw Peninsula.	45
Map 4	Operation Tawakkalna ala Allah	58
Map 5	The final Iraqi offensives into Khuzestan, launched during the summer of 1988.	68

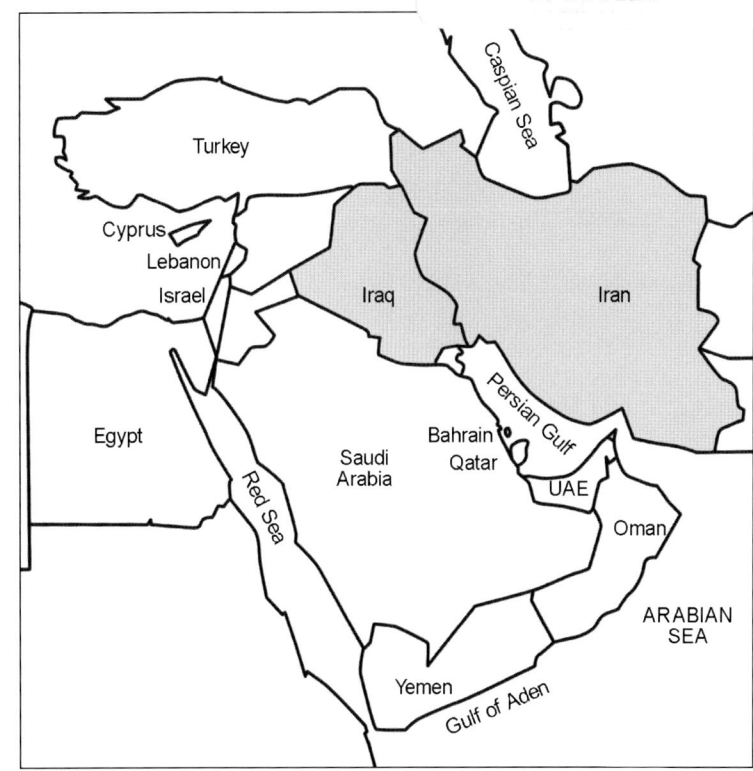

Helion & Company Limited
26 Willow Road, Solihull, West Midlands, B91 1UE, England
Tel. 0121 705 3393
Fax 0121 711 4075
Email: info@helion.co.uk Website: www.helion.co.uk Twitter: @helionbooks Visit our blog http://blog.helion.co.uk/

Published by Helion & Company 2018
Designed and typeset by Farr out Publications, Wokingham, Berkshire
Cover designed by Paul Hewitt, Battlefield Design (www.battlefield-design.co.uk)
Printed by Henry Ling Ltd, Dorchester, Dorset

Text © E. R. Hooton, Tom Cooper & Farzin Nadimi 2017
Photographs © as individually credited
Colour profiles © Tom Cooper 2017

Every reasonable effort has been made to trace copyright holders and to obtain their permission for the use of copyright material. The author and publisher apologize for any errors or omissions in this work, and would be grateful if notified of any corrections that should be incorporated in future reprints or editions of this book.

ISBN 978-1-911512-44-8

British Library Cataloguing-in-Publication Data.
A catalogue record for this book is available from the British Library.

All rights reserved. No part of this publication may be reproduced, stored in a retrieval system, or transmitted, in any form, or by any means, electronic, mechanical, photocopying, recording or otherwise, without the express written consent of Helion & Company Limited.

For details of other military history titles published by Helion & Company Limited contact the above address, or visit our website: http://www.helion.co.uk. We always welcome receiving book proposals from prospective authors.

Acknowledgments

We would like to thank Dr Kevin W. Woods, one of the leading researchers in the Iran-Iraq War, for his extremely useful advice in following certain lines of research; to Major General Aladdin Hussein Makki Khamas for his patient responses and advices to many queries; and to Colonel Pesach Malovany, one of the leading non-Arab authorities on the Iraqi Army, for his assistance and advice.

Note

In order to simplify the use of this book, all names, locations and geographic designations are as provided in *The Times World Atlas*, or other traditionally accepted major sources of reference, as of the time of described events. Similarly, Arabic names are romanised and transcripted rather than transliterated. For example: the definite article al- before words starting with 'sun letters' is given as pronounced instead of simply as al- (which is the usual practice for non-Arabic speakers in most English-language literature and media).

Glossary and abbreviations

AFV	Armoured Fighting Vehicle
AK	Russian for Automat Kalashnikova; general designation for a class of Soviet – or former East Bloc-manufactured class of assault rifles calibre 7.62mm
APC	Armoured Personnel Carrier
AFGC	Armed Forces General Command. Iraqi General headquarters.
ATGM	Anti-tank guided missile
AVBL	Armoured Vehicle Bridge Layer
BRDM	Boyevaya Razvedyvatelnaya Dozornaya Mashina (Combat Reconnaissance Patrol Vehicle). Soviet light AFV.
C3	Command, control and communication.
CAS	Close Air Support
CD	Coast defence
Cdo	Commando
CIA	Central Intelligence Agency (USA)
COIN	Counterinsurgency
CSG/GSG	Combat Support/General Support Groups (IRIAA formations)
ECM	Electronic Counter-Measures
ELINT	Electronic intelligence
FEBA	Forward Edge of Battle Area
FAC	Fast Attack Craft. Small warships with stand-off weapons, torpedoes or more usually surface-to-surface missiles
'Gainful'	ASCC Codename for 2K12 Kub (Cube) surface-to-air missile also designated SA-6
GCAF	General Command of the (Iraqi) Armed Forces
GCHQ	General Command Headquarters (Iraqi)
GMID	General Military Intelligence Directorate (Iraqi)
'Grail'	NATO codename for 9K32 Strela-2, Soviet MANPADS also designated SA-7
'Guideline'	NATO codename for V-750AK Dvina Soviet surface-to-air missile system also designated SA-2e
HE	High Explosive
IFF	Identification Friend or Foe
IFV	Infantry fighting vehicle
Infantry	Infantry
IrAAC	Iraqi Army Aviation Corps
IrAF	Iraqi Air Force
IRI	Islamic Republic of Iran
IRIA	Islamic Republic of Iran Army
IRIAA	Islamic Republic of Iran Army Aviation
IRIAF	Islamic Republic of Iran Air Force
IRIN	Islamic Republic of Iran Navy
IrN	Iraqi Navy
'Kedge A'	NATO codename for laser-guided Russian air-to-surface missile also designated AS-14. Russian designation Kh-29L/ML or 9M721.
'Kyle'	NATO codename for Russian air-to-surface anti-radar missile also designated
AS-9.	Russian designation Kh-28.
LSM	Landing Ship Medium. An amphibious warfare vessel.
MANPADS	Man-Portable Air Defence System. Light surface-to-air missile system which can be carried and deployed in combat by a single soldier
MBT	Main Battle Tank
Mechanised	Mechanised
MHz	Megahertz, millions of cycles per second
MLR	Main Line of Resistance
MLRS	Multiple Launch Rocket System
OPEC	Organization of the Petroleum Exporting Countries
ORBAT	Order of Battle
Pasdaran	Iranian Revolutionary Guards Corps. Members are Pasder.
Polnocny B	Class of Russian-designed landing ship designated Project 773.
RPG	Rocket Propelled Grenade
S-Hour	Arabic for Zero (Sifr) Hour
'Sagger'	NATO codename for Russian anti-armour missile also designated AT-3. Russian designation 9K11 Malyutka (Little One)
SF	Special Forces
SEAL	Sea, Air, Land (Naval Commandos)
SFOH	Southern Forward Operations Headquarters (Iranian)
SIGINT	Signals Intelligence
'Silkworm'	Codename for Chinese-made CHETA HY-2/C.601 Hai Ying (Sea Eagle) anti-ship missile
SNAR	Stantsiya Nazemnoy Artilleriyskoy Razvedki (Artillery Location Radar)
SP	Self propelled (as in artillery) or Special Purpose as in the Republican Guard division
'Spandrel'	NATO codename for Russian anti-armour missile also designated AT-5. Russian designation 9M113 Konkurs (Contest).

'Spigot'	NATO codename for Russian anti-armour missile also designated AT-4. Russian Designation 9K111 Fagot (Bassoon)	TAOR	Tactical Area of Responsibility
		TOW	Tube-launched, Optically-tracked, Wire-guided. American anti-armour missile also designated BGM-71A.
'Swatter'	NATO codename for AT-2A 'Swatter A' or 3M11 Falanga/ AT-2B 'Swatter B' for 9K17 Skorpion (Scorpion).	UAV	Unmanned Aerial Vehicle
		Y-Day	Arabic for D-Day from Yom (Day)

Addenda/Errata to Volumes 1 and 2

Since the publication of Volume 1 the authors have received information correcting some of the statements in earlier works, especially about armoured fighting vehicles, as follows:

(a) While some sources claim Iraq received 400-500 PT-76 tracked reconnaissance vehicles it now appears only a few dozen were delivered and only between 1959 and 1963. Very few of these saw action during the Iran-Iraq War, and then during its first two years only.

(b) T-62 MBTs were delivered to Iraq from 1973 and entered service with the 10th Armoured Brigade. None were acquired after 1980 by when they equipped 3rd, 6th and 10th Armoured Divisions, and one brigade of the 9th Armoured Division. The remainder of 9th Armoured Division and the whole of 12th Armoured Division had T-55s.

(c) After 1980 Iraq acquired only T-72s from Eastern Europe.

(d) In 1980 Iraq bought 1,000 Chinese Type 69 MBTs. A second batch of 1,700 was purchased but only 1,150 were delivered by 1986. Some sources say their Iraqi official designation was T-52 but General Makki stated they were called Chinese T-55s.

(e) Iran received 110 Austrian-made, calibre 155mm GHN-45 towed howitzers and 41,000 shells from Belgium via Libya in 1987.

(f) Iraq received 110 of the same GHN-45 towed guns and 41,000 shells in 1984 and, in 1987, 124 of the similar Denel G-5s. Orders were placed for another 100 G-5 and 90 GHN-45 but most were never delivered.

(g) In 1986 Iran received twenty 170mm Koksan M1978 self-propelled guns from North Korea.

(h) In Volume 1, p.4 Saddam is described as 'Foreign Minister'. He was, in fact, Deputy President

(i) In Volume 1, p.11 the range of the M-110's 203mm howitzer should have read 16.8 kilometres

(j) In Volume 1, p.15 the BTR-60 and BMP-1 were used by both sides. This BTR-60 appears to be an Iranian vehicle.

(k) IRIAA pilot Keshvari, shown in Volume 1, p.21 was killed when his helicopter was shot down over Ilam Province by IrAF aircraft.

(l) Volume 1, p.23 should have noted that the 151st Fortress Battalion of the Iranian Army had only half of its 1,330 authorised strength.

A rare photograph of one of the few PT-76s operated by the Iraqi Army in the 1980-1981 period. The use of troops wearing orange berets indicates its assignment to one of the 'commando' or 'special forces' units. (via Ali Tobchi)

(m) The ERC-TH Hot shown in Volume 1, p.30 was a captured vehicle in Iranian hands.

(n) The ZSU-57-2 shown in Volume 1, p.74 has original Iranian Army markings.

(o) The BMP-1 shown in Volume 1, p.75 appears to have been one of the vehicles transferred to the Pasdaran by the IRIA.

One of at least 110 GHN-45 155mm guns that Iraq obtained from Austria via Belgium, in the period 1984-1987. (Photo by Ted Hooton)

1
IRAN'S LAST CHANCE

Iraq's fortunes were at a nadir after Iran captured the southern Faw Peninsula in Operation 'Valfajr-8' and this was reflected in pessimistic briefings from the US Central Intelligence Agency (CIA). Looking at the implications the Agency noted on 12 March 1986: 'The situation is more ominous for Baghdad than at any time in the struggle.'[1] The same document further said that the already low Iraqi morale might decline further under the burden of heavy casualties and added:

> In any event the initiative now belongs to Iran, but Tehran must act soon, otherwise chances for success will diminish as Baghdad recovers and builds new defenses.

The CIA's assessment continued with observation that further Iranian attacks could lead to a series of setbacks for the overstretched Iraqi Army (IrA), which in turn could collapse and cause the fall of the regime, and concluded that Tehran might be able to hold its gains indefinitely:

> Even if Iran is pushed out of Al Faw eventually, it could make this so costly in manpower and equipment for Baghdad that the Iraqi Army would be seriously weakened.[2]

A fortnight later, another of the CIA's assessment asked, 'Is Iraq Losing the War?' and suggested the answer was positive – if Baghdad continued to pursue the objective of ending rather than winning the war.[3] The perspicacity of CIA analysts would be variously demonstrated or undermined over the next two years, but the tone was undoubtedly reflected in chancelleries and intelligence agencies all over the world.

Meanwhile, from the late summer of 1986 the Iranians spoke openly of preparing for a new offensive, with Speaker Hojatolislam Ali Akbar Rafsanjani claiming on 10 September the

A reconnaissance photograph taken by an RF-4E Phantom II reconnaissance fighter of the IRIAF, showing the Karbala-4 area of operations. The point of crossing of the Karoun River (left) and Shatt al-Arab waterways. (Farzin Nadimi Collection)

Another reconnaissance photograph taken on the same occasion. The arrows show the launching points of Iranian forces. The residential area visible at the centre of the photograph is Abadan, with parts of Khorramshahr also visible at the bottom left. (Farzin Nadimi Collection)

An Iraqi-operated S-60 57 mm anti-aircraft gun, in position east of Basra in 1986 or 1987. Notable is the elaborate network of trenches and bunkers around its sangar. (Tom Cooper Collection)

current mobilisation would be completed within four days. On 16 September Iran's Supreme Leader, Ayatollah Ruhollah al-Musavi al-Khomeini received senior army officers and leaders of the Islamic Revolutionary Guards Corps (IRGC, also 'Pasdaran'), all leave was cancelled while medical facilities through-out the country were placed on the alert. Five days later President Ali Hosseini Khamenei publicly spoke of exploiting the Majnoon oil fields if Iraq failed to provide restitution for war damage, and with 600,000 men at the front it was widely believed that the offensive would be launched on 22 September, the sixth anniversary of the Iraqi invasion.

But that day saw only a huge parade in Tehran, although the Iranians began a series of probes in the Marshes the following day. These soon petered out and the opening of the rainy season at the beginning of November washed away the immediate threat.[4] In fact the rains exacerbated the Iranians' tactical problems because the Iraqis had flooded a 20 kilometre long strip covering the southern approaches to the Fish Lake Line to the international border, and a further 10 kilometres into Iranian territory. Iran's bombastic claims were no cunning plan to confuse the Iraqis, but rather reflected the turmoil within Tehran over the operational planning.[5]

The Great Barrier; The Fish Lake Line

The greatest Iranian problem was to overcome the strongest fortifications in the Middle East, the 20-25 kilometres deep Fish Lake Line. Two writers noted that from the air,

… could be seen the gun parks and the bunkers, the 'scrapes' bulldozed out to protect vehicles, the raised dykes topped with tarmac roads ….(and the)… secondary defensive lines out of interlocking circular positions, laagers of earth with tanks and artillery inside …[6]

The backbone remained the so-called Fish Lake, but the Iraqis had learned the folly of trying to defend the frontiers during 'Ramadan al-Mubarak' in 1982. In the following 50 months the defences around this anti-armour feature were expanded as 400 million cubic metres of heavy clay were excavated at a cost equivalent to $1 billion. The defences were based upon berms, earth embankments 2-3 metres high and 200-800 metres apart, with the removed earth creating a ditch which hindered infantry and AFV attacks. The height of the berm provided good fields of fire and effective defence even if the surrounding area was flooded in the rainy season.[7]

The back-stop positions north of the lake were expanded to create a belt of berm-based battalion positions in a right-angle shape, many of these strong-points having ramps onto which main battle tanks (MBTs) or infantry fighting vehicles (IFVs) could be driven to augment the defenders' fire-power. The strong-points were at the centre of improvised command, control and communication (C3) systems using battlefield surveillance radars, ground movement detectors and image intensifiers to provide early warning of attack. This belt consisted of 27 triangular battalion strong-points, organised chequer-board style, between a pair of roads to provide rapid movement of reserves. The northern part of the belt facing the

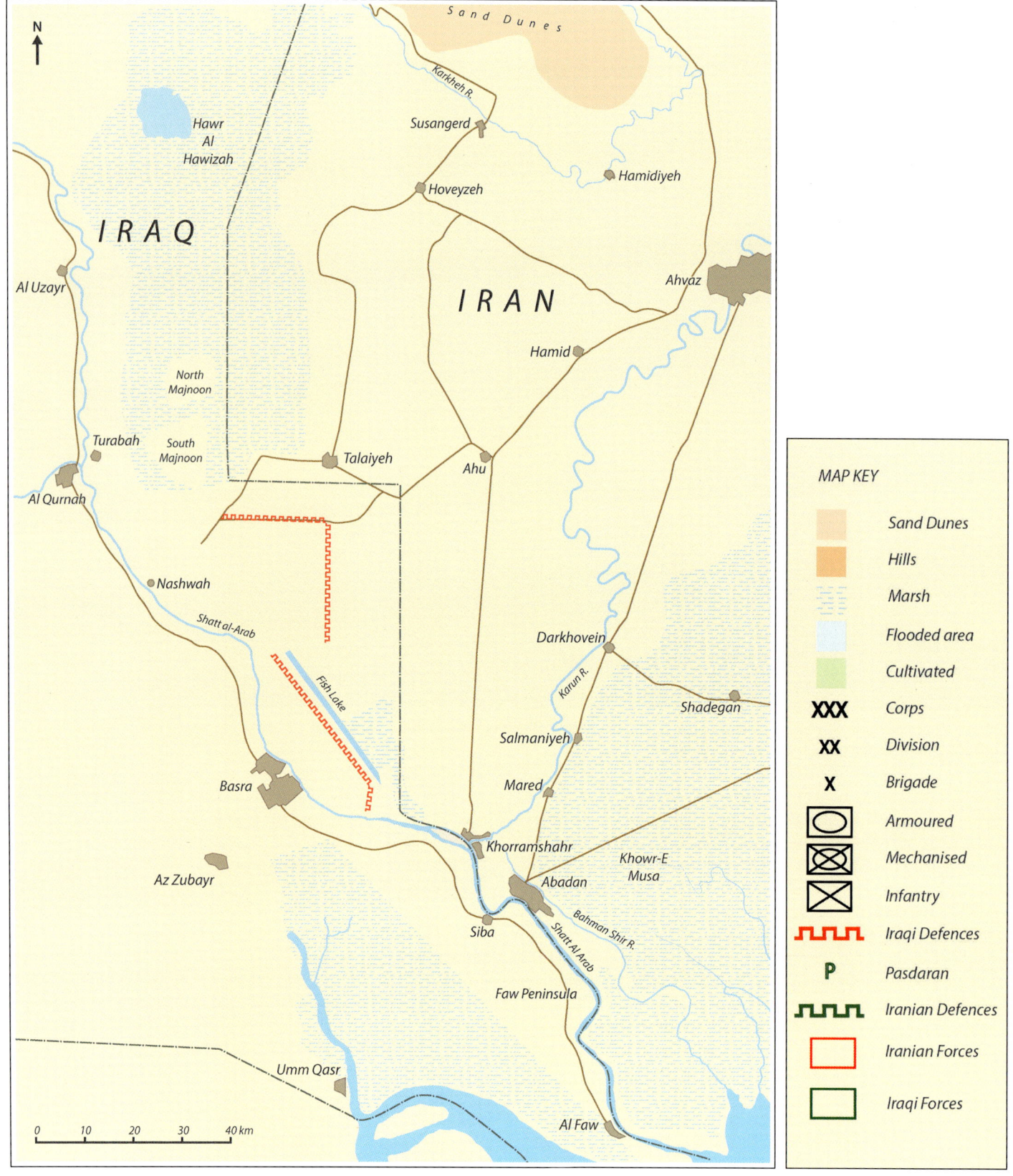

Map 1: The Fish Lake Line.

Marshes had 15 strong-points, while the eastern element consisted of 12 strong-points which 'overhung' the northern approaches to the Fish Lake. In each case two company positions were on the frontline berm covered by a third company position in the rear. Many strong-points augmented infantry weapons with light anti-aircraft guns such as the ZSU-23-4, a 23 mm self-propelled quad gun, which could prove devastating against infantry. These positions also helped to shield the water pumping stations at the head of the Fish Lake.

In front of them, covered by outpost positions, were at least half a kilometre of minefields and wire obstacles, barbed wire fences or single coils of barbed wire. The original minefields were some 350 metres deep, but they were steadily extended to 600 metres with a mine for every metre; a quarter of the mines being anti-armour while the remainder were anti-personnel, notably Italian 'bouncing' mines.[8]

About a dozen strong-points were constructed along the lake's western bank, especially covering the 8-metre-wide causeways designed for Iraqi mechanised counter-attacks, with another three strong-points and two anti-armour ditches providing in-depth defence of the Iraqi entrances. South of the waterway, and bisecting the Basra-Khorramshahr highway, were lines of semi-circular company strong-points, often with 5-metre walls, stretching into the cultivated area which ran along the Shatt. This defensive belt was some 10 kilometres long and 6 kilometres deep with each berm line fronted by a waterway; either an enlarged irrigation channel or a small tributary of the Shatt such as the Rivers al-Duaiji (also 'Da'iji/Diaiji/Du'ayji/Du'ayi/Doeeji') and Jasim ('Jasem'). Behind the fortifications were a myriad of berm-based positions; laagers for mechanised reserves, fire bases for tube and rocket artillery, headquarters and supply dumps, all linked by a growing web of hard- and gravel-topped roads, usually on embankments, for reserves supported by 9P148 Konkurs anti-armour vehicles with two AT-4 'Spigot' or three AT-5 'Spandrel' anti-armour missiles. The artillery had a dedicated communications network, and it is reported that the Iraqi Army had some Soviet 'Pork Trough' (SNAR-2) counter-battery radars as well as British Cymbeline counter-mortar radars.

The southern flanks of these defences were covered by garrisons in company strong-points on the narrow islands of the northern Shatt. West of Umm Rassas was Umm Twaila (or Tawila or Tuwayiah or Omotiavil) which extended past the defences covering the highway, and Umm Salhia (or Ujayrawihah or Salehieh) which reached almost the outskirts of Basra. They were described by Aldridge as 'sandbanks' and separated by a narrow and shallow creek. Approaching these fortifications, the attacker had first to navigate through inundations with a kilometre-wide zone extending from the Hawizah Marshes (Hawr al Hawizah) around the Zayed (also Zayd and Zaid) Salient. To the south were other inundations which extended some 20 kilometres northwards from the Shatt to cover most of the area between the southern Fish Lake, which merged with this zone in the south, and into Iranian territory north of the Basra-Khorramshahr highway, to create an area of some 200 square kilometres.

The northern bank of the Shatt was the weak point of Basra's shield. The frontier ran north-to-south almost to the Shatt, but along the bank was an Iraqi salient. This was literally an island with inundations to the north and east, and the Shatt to the south, while from the Fish Lake canals designed to control flooding ran down to the Shatt. The groves on both sides of the Shatt had made Iraq the world's prime producer of dates, but farmers had long abandoned this fertile strip and years of war had left the groves with blackened and broken palm trees.[9] The flooding was deep enough to slow infantry but shallow enough in places to cause assault boats to run aground. The edges of the inundated area were lined with multiple lines of wire entanglements, liberally laced with mines, and with electrodes linked to Basra's electric power stations; all covered by shallow trench positions.

Overcoming defences on this scale was not impossible and, since 1917, has been achieved with or without significant armoured support. Beginning with short, overwhelming artillery bombardments upon a narrow front; these were rapidly followed by assaults involving combined-arms groups operating flexibly to infiltrate, isolate and then overwhelm surviving positions. The Coalition Forces demonstrated this in 1991, with the added support of precision-guided munitions. However, five years earlier the Iranians lacked both skills and weaponry, and it was unclear how would they – already suffering serious shortages of heavy weapons and ammunition – achieve this goal.[10]

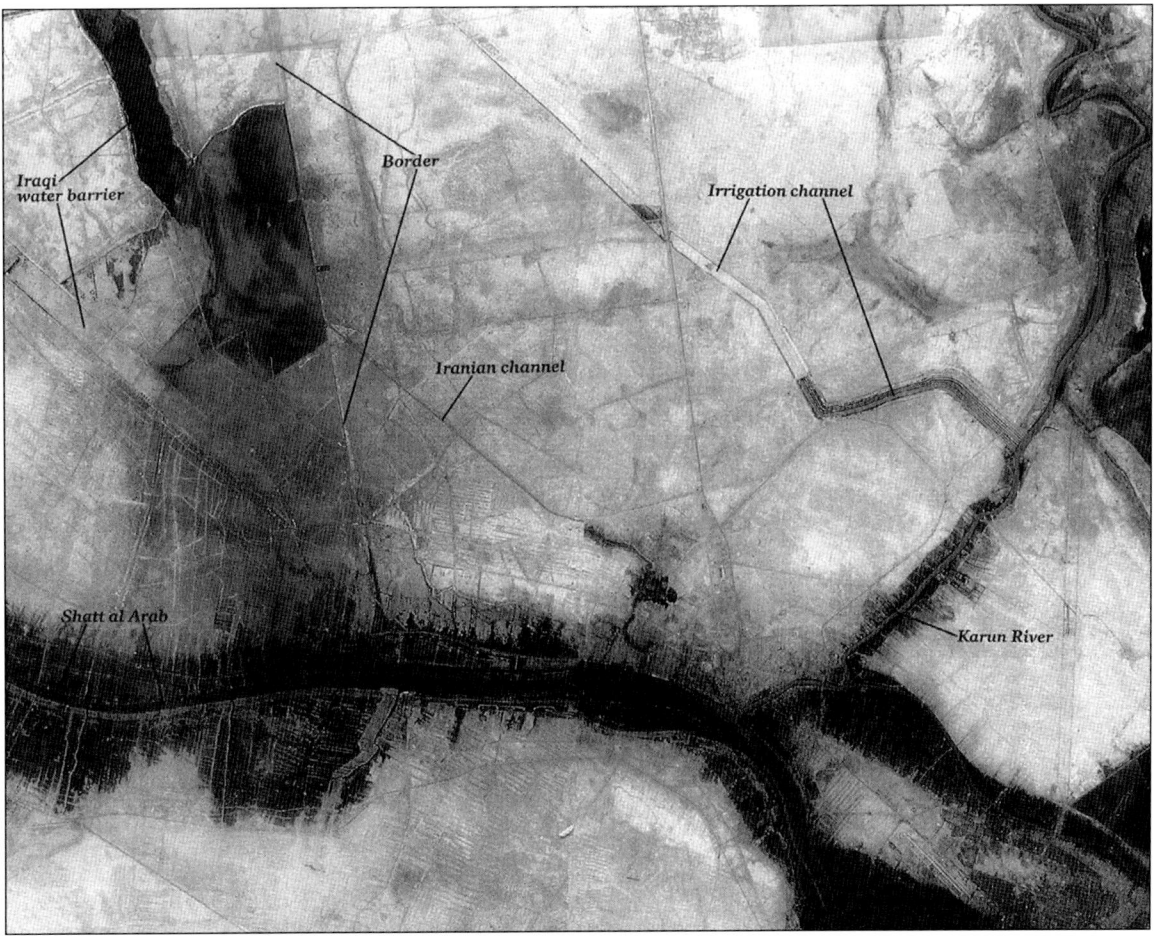

A SPOT satellite photograph (as used by Iranians for their operational planning), from September 1987, showing the area between Fish Lake (left upper corner), Shatt al-Arab and the Karoun River – the centrepiece of Iranian offensives in 1987. (Tom Cooper Collection)

A view into the Khatam al-Anbia headquarters of the Iranian forces. Notable is a large wall-map, made of reconnaissance photographs taken by IRIAF and SPOT satellites. (Tom Cooper Collection)

While often dehumanised and belittled as 'cockroaches' running 'human wave attacks', and certainly poorly trained, the Pasdaran infantry proved one of the most effective 'arms' of the Iranian military and were much feared even by Iraqi generals. Here an IRGC officer is briefing his troops before the next operation. (Tom Cooper Collection)

Target: Basra

In the aftermath of Valfajr-8 Iran's Supreme Defence Council (SDC) agreed that the strategic level objective should be to take Basra, a predominantly Shi'a city. Correspondingly, from May to August 1986 military leaders conducted a series of operational level studies to determine ways of cracking the city's defences. The 'maximalists', led by Pasdaran commander Mohsen Rezai, wanted a frontal assault from the east to bulldoze through the Fish Lake defences. The 'minimalists', led by the commander of the Islamic Republic of Iran Army (IRIA), Colonel Ali Sayad Shirazi, were more cautious: they pointed out the strong defences and overwhelming enemy superiority in armour, artillery and air power compared with Iranian inferiority in all three. Shirazi, who appears to have had some support within the Pasdaran, wanted a well-planned, well-co-ordinated, two-prong offensive; one by the IRIA from the Hawizah Marshes southwards against, and around, the Fish Lake Line; and the second by the Pasdaran along the Faw Peninsula following an amphibious assault across the Shatt. However, the problems experienced by the Iranians while striking from the Hawizah Marshes, demonstrated by 'Kheiber' and 'Badr', forced the IRIA to accept an assault upon the Fish Lake Line from the east as one element, and in conjunction with an attack from the Faw Peninsula.

While the Pasdaran were willing to accept the IRIA's indirect concept, they believed in the supremacy of their men's revolutionary and religious fervour and demanded a greater share in the enterprise. There was no doubt that some of their leaders recognised that they were materially handicapped and they accepted the truth of the IRIA's demands for greater Pasdaran professionalism to augment revolutionary zeal. Nevertheless, dispute developed: this tore apart old alliances and brought Shirazi into an increasingly vitriolic conflict with Rezai. According to different reports, at one point in time they came to blows.[11] Shirazi insisted on improving overall direction by introducing Army standards of planning and preparation, but the clerics naturally favoured Rezai over any professional military officer, no matter how devout and devoted. Ultimately, Shirazi was dismissed on 4 August 1986 in favour of Southern Forward Operational Headquarters (SFOH) commander, Colonel Hossein Hassani-Sa'di, who had directed 'Valfajr-8'.

It was thus the Pasdaran influence that resulted in the plan – placed before the SDC on 8 September – which called for simultaneous attacks along and across the Shatt. This was formally accepted in October but became subject to clerical and political tinkering with demands for the offensive to coincide with the Islamic Summit Congress scheduled in December in Kuwait. Brigadier Qasem Ali Zahirnejad (Khomeinei's representative in the SDC), and Armed Forces Chief-of-Staff Colonel Ismail Sohrabi, together with President Khamenei, wished to strike earlier. Furthermore, the Pasdaran, backed by Rafsanjani, persuaded Khomeini that the offensive would strengthen Iran's status in the Islamic World, and thus the overall command was given to the IRGC's Haj Ahmad Kosari.

Rafsanjani was a strident advocate for the offensive – foremost because this was likely to offset his support for the secret 'Irangate' arms-for-hostages-deal with the United States. The details had been revealed as the radicals jockeyed for position in the run-up to the parliamentary elections scheduled for the spring of 1988 when no-one could afford to be seen as 'soft.' Khomeini was obviously ill and politicians were staking out their post-mortem positions. While Rafsanjani was the leading candidate to replace the Ayatollah as head of state, there was another contender for the position of Khomeini's successor as religious leader: Ayatollah Husseini Ali Montazeri. Montazeri's relative and Pasdaran Chief-of-Staff, Mehdi Hashemi, revealed details of 'Irangate' in public with the aim of giving Montazeri's opponents the excuse to arrest 200 of his supporters, in October 1986. In turn, Hashemi was tried and convicted of treason on 10 December. One commentator observed that this would explain why the offensive 'proved to be the worst managed Iranian attack since Iran's offensives in 1984.[12] In December various Iranian politicians demanded the offensive be brought forward to put greater pressure upon the Arabs during the summit in Kuwait: certainly enough, they had also been seeking a public diversion from the purge of Montazeri's supporters.

With the end of the harvest, Tehran planned to create 500 new Basij 'battalions' with 100,000 men to fill out the Pasdaran formations. However, only 300 of these (including about 60,000 combatants) were actually established.[13] Even Rafsanjani had no desire to throw untrained men at enemy fortifications and demanded that the Basiji be given up to a year's training – although they usually received only three months before mobilisation and up to three months at the front.

Operation Karbala-4 (al-Yawm al-Adheem)

By December 1986 some 200,000 men (13 divisions) were concentrated north of the Shatt, of whom 60% were Pasdaran and Basiji. The new offensive was designated Operation Karbala-4 and envisaged the Shatt al Arab itself being the main axis of attack towards Basra. It would include a direct attack from south of Shalamcheh across the Shatt, where the Iran-Iraq border follows the waterway. Another prong was to follow up the Basra Khorramshahr highway. The amphibious assault would repeat Valfajr-8, with bridgeheads re-established opposite Umm al-Rassas ('Om al-Rasas' or 'Omorrasas' in Farsi) – the long island running from opposite Khorramshahr to opposite the frontier. The Iranians may have had a second stage contingency plan to exploit success in the northern Faw Peninsula with a second cross-Shatt assault from Minoo ('Minu') Island. This was intended to help the besieged troops in the Faw Peninsula bridgehead to fight their way northwards and increase the southern threat to Basra. To divert enemy attention there would be a heliborne landing in the Umm Qasr area, at which two Scud missiles would also be fired during the operation. The initial Iranian objective on the south bank of the Shatt was the ruined refinery complex of Abu al-Khasib, west of the River Abu Fulus (or Abu Floos), whose capture would allow them to enfilade the defences south of the Fish Lake.

Task Forces Najaf and Quds would strike north of the Shatt, the former was north of the flooded area, while the latter would strike along the highway. The Shatt would be crossed by Task Force Karbala from the Khorramshahr area (this included 18 brigades of the IRIA and the IRGC, with 52,000 troops), leap-frogging the Shatt islands, and Nooh from Minoo Island south of Abadan (the latter included 14 brigades with 49,000 troops, supported by two artillery- and two engineer brigades of the Pasdaran; see Table 1 for order of battle). The Islamic Republic of Iran Army Aviation (IRIAA) provided 112 helicopters – including 24 Bell AH-1 Cobra gunships – to support this operation. The prospects for the landing were good as the channel is less than half a kilometre wide, narrower where it is constrained by the islands, and the water moves slowly so that once the bridgehead was secured a pontoon bridge could be thrown across.

The concept was essentially what 'Valfajr-8' might have been – if the clerics had seriously intended to strike towards Basra – but it suffered the same serious deficiencies as the earlier operation. If the Pasdaran established bridgeheads they would require rapid reinforcement and heavy weapons to reach Basra in the face of Iraqi artillery deployed at the Fish Lake Line. The same would also be able to engage the northern thrust which would have to cross the inundations before reaching the Line's outposts.

Because the Iranians expected a massive reaction from the Iraqi Air Force (IrAF), and knew they could expect little support from the exhausted Islamic Republic of Iran Air Force (IRIAF), they established a significant concentration of ground-based air defence assets, including five MIM-23B I-HAWK battalions of surface-to-air missiles (SAMs). These were augmented by two British-made Rapier systems, anti-aircraft artillery units including 30 Oerlikon 35mm guns supported by 10 Sky Guard radars, and the IRGC's 95th Moharram Air Defence Brigade.

As with Valfajr-8 there was an extensive reconnaissance effort involving McDonnell-Douglas RF-4E Phantom II reconnaissance jets of the IRIAF, special forces of the IRIA, Pasdaran scouts and even UAVs. But the IrAF, possibly cued by US Intelligence reports based upon satellite imagery, was also conducting its own reconnaissance effort and on 23 December brought back photographs of major enemy troop concentrations facing III and VII Corps.[14] Anticipating an assault, starting in mid-October 1986, the IrAF began interdicting communications and concentrations in the Khorramshahr-Abadan area: such attacks proved highly effective and eroded Iranian military engineering and road construction capabilities by 75-85 per cent.[15]

On 22 December 1986 the General Military Intelligence Directorate of Iraq (GMID) reported the enemy had forward-deployed 25 helicopters and that they had completed preparations for an offensive in the south.[16] Baghdad therefore placed its forces on alert and the IrAF – flying up to 194 fixed-wing sorties – heavily bombed the whole assembly area and continued to do so until 26 December 1986. Many of the attacks in question were flown by Tupolev Tu-22 bombers of No. 18 and No. 36 Squadrons, IrAF, which made extensive use of the heaviest bombs in Iraqi arsenal, like the 3000kg FAB-3000 and 9000kg FAB-9000.[17]

Battle of the Red Night

With the Iraqis on full alert the Iranians were left without a choice but to move out. At 22:30 on 23 December 1986, they launched their assault over formidable obstacles. To reach the Fish Lake Line their infantry first had to cross a flooded area 2-3 kilometres wide to reach the frontier, then 4 kilometres of dry land, before forcing its way across four small rivers each backed by a fortified berm. Across the Shatt, the VII Corps of the Iraqi Army, commanded by Lieutenant General Maher Abd al-Rashid ('Maher'), had already created a killing zone along the northern coast of the Faw Peninsula opposite Umm Rassas and Umm Al Jababi (Omolbabi) with bunkers, watch towers, barbed wire entanglements and mines

Table 1: Order of Battle for Operation Karbala-4, December 1986		
Corps	**Division**	**Brigades**
Iran		
Task Force Najaf	92nd Armoured Division IRIA	2 brigades
	3rd Sahel ol-Zaman Division IRGC	3 brigades
	7th Vali Asr Division IRGC	3 brigades
	31st Ashura Division IRGC	3 brigades
Task Force Qods	5th Nasr Division IRGC	3 brigades
	10th Seyyed ash-Shohada Division IRGC	3 brigades
	17th Ali Ibn Abu Talib Division IRGC	3 brigades
	33rd al-Mahdi Division IRGC	2 brigades
	41st Sarallah Division IRGC	3 brigades
	57th Abolfazl al-Abbas Division IRGC	3 brigades
	16th al-Hadi Brigade IRGC	
	48th Fath al-Mustaqil Brigade IRGC	
Task Force Karbala	92nd Armoured Division IRIA	1 brigade
	21st Infantry Division IRIA	2 brigades
	14th Imam Hossein Division IRGC	3 brigades
	25th Karbala Division IRGC	3 brigades
	27th Mohammad Rasoolallah Division IRGC	3 brigades
	32nd Ansar al-Hossein Division IRGC	3 brigades
	33rd al-Mahdi Division IRGC	1 brigade
	64th Suduqu Brigade IRGC	
	106th Sajjad Naval Brigade IRGC	
Task Force Nooh	8th Najaf Ashraf Division IRGC	3 brigades
	19th Fajr Division IRGC	3 brigades
	21st Imam Reza Division IRGC	3 brigades
	30th Beit-ol-Moghaddas Division IRGC	3 brigades
	104th Amir al-Mo'menin Brigade IRGC	
	105th Kowsar Naval Brigade IRGC	
Support Forces	22nd Artillery Group IRIA	
	33rd Artillery Group IRIA	
	90th Khatam al-Anbiya Artillery Brigade IRGC	
	91st Hadid Artillery Brigade IRGC	
	40th Sahel az-Zaman Engineer Battalion IRGC	
	43rd Imam Ali Engineer Battalion IRGC	
	2nd Combat Support Group IRIAA	
	3rd Combat Support Group IRIAA	
	4th General Support Group IRIAA	
Iraq		
VII Corps	1st & 2nd Commando Brigades, VII Corps Artillery Brigade	corps troops
	15th Infantry Division	22nd, 104th, 111th, 238th, 436th, 702nd, 802nd Infantry Brigades
	6th Armoured Division	25th Mechanised Brigade
III Corps	1st & 2nd Commando Brigades, III Corps Artillery Brigade	
	11th Infantry Division	23rd, 45th, 47th, 81st, 421st, 422nd, 429th, 501st Infantry Brigades
	3rd Wing IrAAC	

While often belittled by foreign observers, Iraqi Tu-22 operations were very intensive during several periods of the war with Iran. They included the bombardment of major assembly points of the Iranian ground forces with some of heaviest bombs of Soviet- and Iraqi manufacture. (Tom Cooper Collection)

Officers of one of the IRGC's naval brigades, leaning on one of countless earthen berms constructed by both sides, trying to make out Iraqi positions and intentions opposing them. (Farzin Nadimi Collection)

Pasdaran of Imam Hossein Division at their gathering point near Jufayr, east of Basra. (Photo by M. H.)

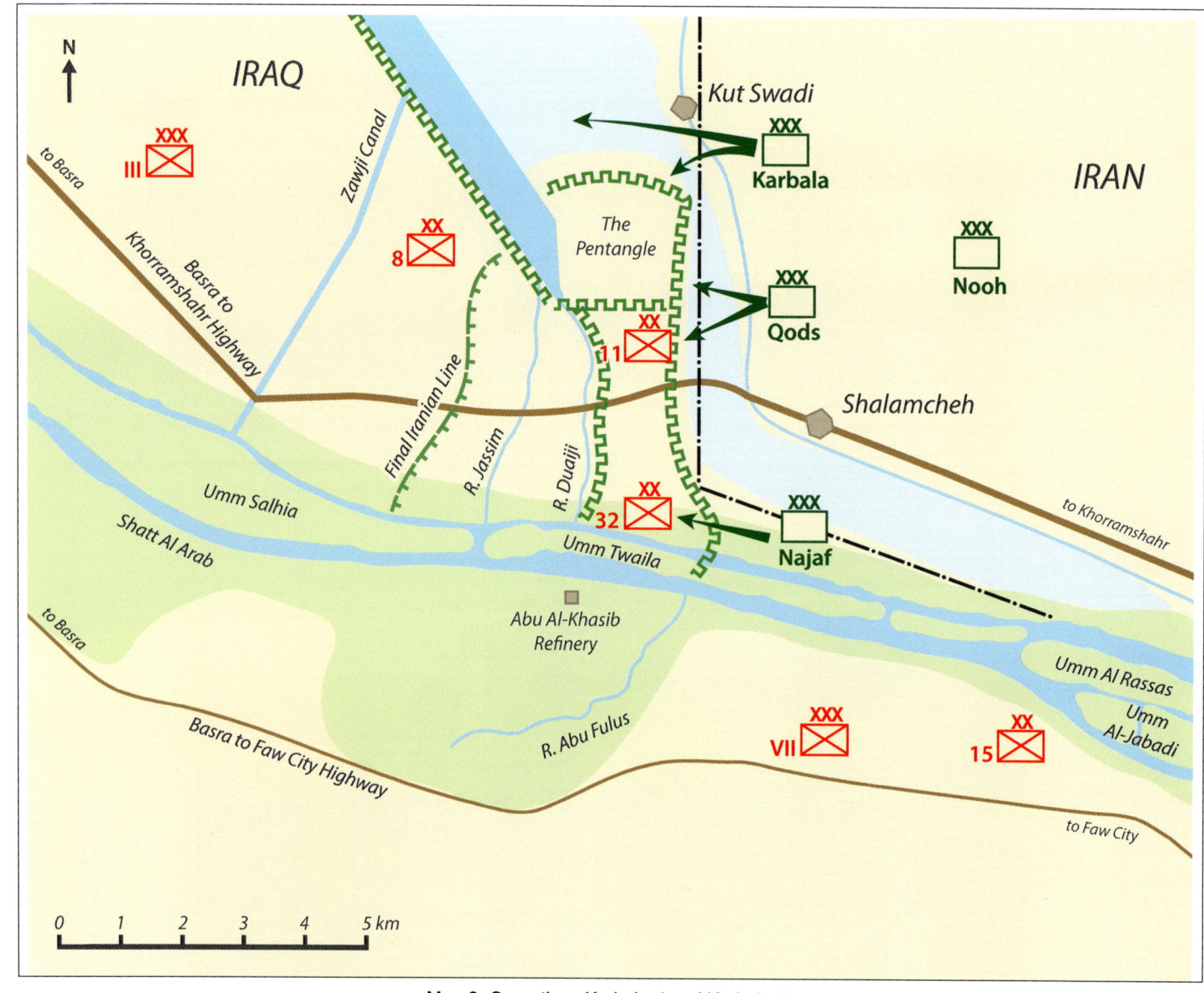

Map 2: Operations Karbala-4 and Karbala-5.

amid the date palm groves.[18] His northern sector was still held by Brigadier Qays Muhammad Ali's 15th Infantry Division, which had seven brigades opposite the Iranian bank, with the 104th Infantry Brigade holding the islands, and reserves of a mechanised brigade, reconnaissance and divisional commando battalions. These were supported by 15 corps batteries giving the 28,000 men some 160 guns and a FROG battery.

The operation was opened by an assault of frogmen and SEALs of Sajjad Brigade IRGC, across the waters to Umm Rassas and Umm al-Jababi, in fibre-glass assault craft and rubber dinghies. On the western side of the waterway, the Iranians were caught totally exposed and machine-gunned in a hail of bullets. About 175 were killed: some of them only after being caught and then buried alive without injuries, but with their hands tied.[19]

The second wave followed with grim determination, landing a blow on the 104th Infantry Brigade and taking the defenders by surprise. Contrary to their usual tactics, the Pasdaran made little attempt to infiltrate the defences. Instead, they resorted to piecemeal frontal attacks, exposing themselves to murderous cross-fire that caused terrible loss of life among the massed men and follow-on forces. They gained a foothold on the River Abu Fulus, but then became struck in between Iraqi defences, hamstrung as much by the haphazard preparation as by minimum support from their own artillery and that of the regular Army. The reed beds provided little cover, while many boats were sunk or smashed and reduced the flow of reinforcements to a trickle. Early the next morning, a combination of Iraqi air strikes, helicopter attacks and artillery barrages smothered the Iranian guns on the far side of the Shatt al-Arab. Lacking electronic countermeasures to penetrate dense Iraqi air defences, the IRIAF was only able to provide 23 attack sorties; none of these deeper than 8 kilometres behind the front-line. On the contrary, the intensity of the Iraqi artillery fire 'turned night into day' – which is why this became known as the battle of 'The Red Night'.

The Iraqis then launched counter-attacks that regained part of Umm al-Arassas, while containing the threat to the offshore islands. Finally, an attack by elements of 6th Armoured Division and the 66th Special Forces Brigade, from the morning of 25 December 1986, drove the enemy into the water.

The Glorious Day

Task Force Karbala's failure meant that Task Force Nooh's operations were confined to some brief, half-hearted, probes by two naval brigades on the far bank of the Shatt before being abandoned. On the north bank of the Shatt, the assault upon Major General Tali Khalil Ruhayyim al-Duri's III Corps fell, once more, on 11th was explained with 'attempts to destroy enemy artillery on the south bank of the Shatt'. Rafsanjani – still convinced of the value of mass attacks – launched a hunt for scapegoats and blamed the country's military leaders. Nevertheless another, even deadlier, offensive was to follow in a matter of two weeks.[20]

Operation Karbala-5 (al-Hassad al-Akbar)

The Karbala-4 disaster should have been a wake-up call for the Iranian leadership: instead, Iranian accounts indicate it 'plunged the Supreme Command into crisis'.[21] To the 'hawks', the best way to achieve their dreams and destroy Iraq continued to be a direct offensive upon Basra, as espoused by IRGC's leader Mohsen Rezai. Hassani-Sa'di's position was unclear but his experience in 'Valfajr-8' was likely to have made him more sympathetic to the IRIA viewpoint.[22]

Basra remained a prime objective both as a large, historic city and port whose loss would undermine Saddam's prestige. He would clearly wish to hold it at all costs and this provided the Iranians with a good opportunity to grind down the Iraqi army. However, top leaders in Tehran were becoming acutely aware of the fact that their country possessed finite resources. As Rafsanjani put it:

'In our opinion, there exists no other solution better than accelerating the war operations based on our calculations made so far. The country's general situation and its economic conditions imply bringing this problem to an ultimate point as soon as possible.'

Pressure to end the war was fed by the Iraqi air and missile offensive in the 'War of the Cities', which was eroding Iranian morale amid growing demands for an end to the threat. Tehran's prime objective remained the destruction of the Iraqi war machine and demoralisation of Saddam's regime, while Shi'a clerics hoped to force out Basra's Sunni inhabitants and replace them with 500,000 Iraqi Shia exiles and refugees when they occupied the city. Furthermore, Iranian leaders were determined not to let the enemy regain the initiative – especially not on the Faw Peninsula – and were hoping to exploit winter's heavy rains to restrict enemy superiority in the air and in armour. Unsurprisingly, for the new offensive – code-named 'Karbala-5' – the IRGC was again to provide the spearhead. On the contrary, the IRIA was expected to 'sit out' an offensive in which it had little confidence except through providing artillery-, engineer-, and helicopter-support.[23]

In what Teheran began claiming would be the 'final battle', the objective was to break the stalemate with an assault on the southern Fish Lake Line, aiming to drain the defenders' lifeblood and allow an advance which would also allow a break-out from the Faw Peninsula bridgehead in direction of Basra. Before the attack Rafsanjani said:

'Our aim is to completely destroy the Iraqi war machine. Here, near Basra, Saddam cannot do anything but fight, for the fall of Basrah is tantamount to his own death. We want to settle our accounts with Iraq at Basra's gates, which will open and pave the way for the final victory we have promised.'

Encouraged by the perceived success of Task Force Najaf during Karbala-4, and based on extensive aerial reconnaissance – including the use of UAVs – detailed planning began on 27 December 1986. However, detailed plans were drafted by the SFOH – or Khatam ol-Anbiya – Headquarters literally on the eve of the assault. Unknown to them, the Iranians were assisted by an error of the US intelligence services: these failed to monitor adequately sales of the specialized equipment needed to read Land Satellite (Landsat) imagery. This equipment was received in 1986 and allowed the Iranians to use satellite imagery to prepare their offensives.[24]

The successes and failures of operations on this front since 1985

BGM-71A TOW-armed AH-1J Cobra attack helicopters remained the most potent anti-armour asset in the Iranian arsenal throughout the war with Iraq. This example was photographed at a forward base near Ahwaz, in November 1986. (Farzin Nadimi Collection)

Infantry Division (total of eight brigades, augmented by a tank battalion and two commando battalions, supported by 32 batteries of corps artillery, which gave it 25,000 troops with 290 guns). This Iraqi concentration was struck from the north by 11 brigades of Task Force Najaf – which sought to outflank the highway defences from the north – while 89,000 troops of the 19 brigades of Task Force Quds advanced along the highway, or along the waterway's island, supported by two IRIA artillery groups.

Outnumbered 2:1, the Iraqis again relied upon their artillery augmented – at dawn – by air power. The IrAF flew no less than 361 fixed-wing sorties on 25 December 1986, while the Iraqi Army Air Corps (IrAAC) provided 110 rotary-wing sorties. Task Force Najaf did penetrate the northern part of the first defensive line, forcing the Iraqis to withdraw to the second line, but just before noon an Iraqi counter-attack retook the positions after a 14-hour battle. The Iranians retreated back across the inundations covered by 21st IRIA Division (assigned to the Task Force Karbala).

By dusk on 25 December, after 39 hours fighting, it was all over and the Shatt reportedly ran red with blood from between 9,000 and 12,000 Iranian casualties (including only 200 prisoners). The IRIAA lost nine helicopters too. The Iraqis suffered some 3,000 casualties, but were clearly victorious and thus this attack went down in their history as 'The Glorious Day' (al-Yawm al-Adheem). The Iraqi success did much to raise their morale: the Iraqi corps commanders claimed to have killed 83,000, creating a complacent atmosphere in Baghdad, where Saddam Hussein al-Tikriti and his circle believed the enemy would not be capable of any major effort for another six months. In Tehran, the disaster was such that the entire operation

Table 2: Order of Battle for Operation Karbala-5, January 1987

Corps	Division	Brigades
Iran		
Task Force Karbala	14th Imam Hossain Division IRGC	3 brigades
	25th Karbala Division IRGC	3 brigades
	33rd al-Mahdi Division IRGC	3 brigades
	41st Sarallah Division IRGC	3 brigades
	83rd Ramadan Armoured Brigade IRGC	
	18th al-Ghadir Infantry Brigade IRGC	
	16th Armoured Division IRIA	1 brigade
	21st Infantry Division IRIA	2 brigade
	92nd Armoured Division IRIA	1 brigade (3rd)
Task Force Qods	10th Seyed o-Shohada Division IRGC	3 brigades
	17th Ali Ibn Abu Talib Division IRGC	3 brigades
	19th Fajr Division IRGC	3 brigades
	27th Mohammad Rasoolallah Division IRGC	3 brigades, 1 mech. battalion
	32nd Ansar al-Hossein Division IRGC	3 brigades
Task Force Najaf	3rd Saheb az-Zaman Division IRGC	3 brigades
	5th Nasr Division IRGC	3 brigades, 1 mech. battalion
	7th Vali Asr Division IRGC	3 brigades
	21st Imam Reza Division IRGC	3 brigades
	31st Ashura Division IRGC	3 brigades
	155th Shohada Division IRGC	3 brigades
	85th Moharram Mechanised Brigade IRGC	
Task Force Nooh	8th Najaf-Ashraf Division IRGC	3 brigades, 1 mech. battalion
	9th Badr Division IRGC	3 brigades
	57th Abolfazl al-Abbas Division IRGC	3 brigades
	12th Qa'em-e Mohammad Mechanised Division IRGC	2 brigades
	29th Nabi al-Akram Brigade IRGC	
	90th Khatam al-Anbya Artillery Brigade IRGC	
Support Forces	22nd Artillery Group IRIA	
	33rd Artillery Group IRIA	
	90th Khatam al-Anbiya Artillery Brigade IRGC	
	91st Hadid Artillery Brigade IRGC	
	40th Saheb az-Zaman Engineer Brigade IRGC	
	43rd Imam Ali Engineer Brigade IRGC	
	1st Combat Support Group IRIAA	
	2nd Combat Support Group IRIAA	
	3rd Combat Support Group IRIAA	
	4th General Support Group IRIAA	
Iraq		
III Corps	1st & 2nd Commando Brigades, III Corps Artillery Brigade	
	2nd Infantry Division	39th, 116th, 423rd, 435th Infantry Brigades
	8th Infantry Division	3rd, 9th, 22nd, 28th Infantry Brigades
	11th Infantry Division	23rd, 45th, 47th, 81st, 421st, 422nd, 501st Infantry Brigades

	19th Infantry Division	82nd, 108th, 427th Infantry Brigades
	32nd Infantry Division	44th, 48th, 101st, 102nd Infantry Brigades
	1st Mechanised Division	34th Armoured Brigade
	3rd Armoured Division	6th & 12th Armoured Brigades; 8th Mechanised Brigade
	5th Mechanised Division	26th Armoured, 15th & 20th Mechanised Brigades
	12th Armoured Division	37th Armoured & 46th Mechanised Brigade
	6th Armoured Division	25th Mechanised Brigade
	18th, 83rd, 94th, 101st, 478th, 702nd, 703rd, 706th Infantry Brigades	
	65th Special Forces Brigade	
	3rd Wing IrAAC	
AFGC	10th Armoured Division	17th & 42nd Armoured Brigades, 24th Mechanised Brigade
	Medina Manarawah Armoured Division Republican Guards	2nd & 10th Armoured Brigades, 14th Mechanised Brigade, 3rd Commando Brigade Republican Guards
	Baghdad Infantry Division Republican Guards	4th, 5th, 6th, 7th Infantry Brigades Republican Guards
VII Corps	15th Infantry Division	76th Infantry Brigade
	68th Special Forces Brigade	

were carefully examined, and during the summer and autumn exercises were held in the marshes along the Caspian Sea with the aim of determining the most effective way of crossing the flooded zone between the Fish Lake and the border. The involved infantry were well-armed, well-equipped and were led by a large core of experienced junior- and non-commissioned officers, and given very clear briefings of their tactical objectives. Nevertheless, because of the strength of the Iraqi's defences, and Tehran's diminutive artillery train, tactics was rendered subtly irrelevant: instead, the Pasdaran aimed to bulldoze through the southern defences and outflank the Fish Lake.[25] Unsurprisingly, Iranians sources indicate significant unrest among the IRGC's leadership about the prospects of success. The commander of the Imam Hossein Division should have told his men to rely upon their faith for, '…nothing but a miracle will help us!'[26] Furthermore, during a conference of top generals attended by Rezai, on 8 January 1987, Ahmad Gholampour – commander of the Task Force Karbala – laid out the stark choices:
- authorize the offensive immediately before the enemy discovered its imminence, or
- disperse the troops back to their camps.

His objections resulted in 'considerable discussion' between Rezai and his advisors before the order to attack was issued late that night – essentially with the aim of raising political prestige during the Kuwait conference.[27]

For Karbala-5, the Iranians concentrated four corps-sized task forces – Karbala, Qods, Najaf, and Nooh – forces under the command of Khatam ol-Anbiya Headquarters, with some 215,000 men (see Table 2 for an order of battle). Task Force Karbala totalled 18 brigades and 70,000 men that were planned to strike across the broadest part of the inundated area – the point where this merged with the southern Fish Lake – to create bridgeheads on its western bank. Meanwhile, Qods – which totalled 15 brigades and 62,000 troops – was to strike across the narrower inundated area into the exposed Iraqi salient, and then push westwards around the southern edge of the Fish Lake. Once there, it was to link-up with Karbala and advance westwards to Basra. Nineteen brigades of Najaf – a total of about 78,500 troops – was to strike along the northern bank of the Shatt, leaving Nooh in reserve with 12 infantry-, and one of the Pasdaran's artillery brigades (a total of 51,500 troops). All combined, the IRIA and IRGC could contribute about 570 artillery pieces and some 40 multiple rocket launchers to the operation. Further support was to be provided by two Pasdaran engineer brigades and about 250 MBTs from the Army's and Pasdaran's armoured- and mechanised brigades, and mechanised battalions equipped with BTR-50 APCs, variously known as 'Raksh' and 'Kashayar'.[28] The IRIAA assembled a record number of 131 helicopters, including 28 Cobra gunships (only 10 of these armed with BGM-71 TOW anti-tank guided missiles), to provide much-needed direct support, and 12 Boeing CH-47C Chinook transport helicopters to bring in supplies and reinforcements as well as evacuating wounded.[29]

Overall, there was little doubt that Karbala-5 was a hastily-arranged gamble, lacking crucial fire-support and armour – despite an attempt to increase helicopter support. Its success depended upon flexible execution and close co-operation between the IRIAA and the IRGC. The latter was next to impossible, especially considering that even the headquarters of different Task Forces rarely communicated between each other: instead, they relied upon the SFOH for coordination. Unrecognized by the Iranians was also the fact that the flooded terrain largely restricted their deployment along the Basra-Khorramshahr highway – the key to supporting the main assault – in turn creating a situation similar to that which faced the British XXX Corps in September 1944 during Operation Market Garden. Correspondingly, the Iranian thrust was exposed not only to fire from the west and the north but also from the south across the Shatt, and to the fire from Iraqi positions on the islands, while the assault force was weakened because five divisions had been battered only a fortnight earlier and had barely received replacements.

Nevertheless, preparations went ahead and were largely successful thanks to thick cloud cover and then dense fog, starting with 7 January 1987. These helped conceal resulting troop concentrations from US reconnaissance satellites.

Ya-Zahra!

The signal for the start of the attack, 'Ya-Zahra', was transmitted by the SFOH at 01:00 on 9 January 1987; with the offensive scheduled to start at 02:00 after clouds obscured the moon. Around midnight it began to rain, yet when an officer of the 'Imam Reza' Division expressed his concerns about the change in weather to his divisional commander it was suggested that the rain was a blessing from God.[30]

In front of this unit was the III Corps of the Iraqi Army – still under the incompetent Duri, whose territory of operations extended across the Shatt to cover the area opposite the Shalamcheh and the offshore islands. Duri had no less than 130,000 troops of the 2nd, 8th, 11th, 19th and 32nd Infantry Divisions. These held the main frontline, with the 3rd Armoured Division and the 5th Mechanised Division and several commando brigades in reserve. Further behind was the 10th Armoured Division (behind the Fish Lake), officially assigned to the Armed Forces General Command (AFGC).

Holding the southern part of Fish Lake was 8th Infantry Division (Brigadier Nawfal Ismail Khudayyir), while 32nd Infantry Division (Brigadier Dawood Salman) held the offshore islands and the northern shore of the Faw Peninsula.

Unknown to the Iraqis was that the main Iranian blow would again fall upon 11th Infantry Division, now under command of the future Chief-of-Staff of the Iraqi Army, Brigadier Abdul Wahid Shannan ar-Rabat ('Shannan'). This unit still totalled about 24,000 men in eight infantry brigades. The main position of this unit was just east of the bottom of the Fish Lake and called 'The Pentangle' (Panj-zelee) by the Iranians. This area – its eastern side leaning on the Lake, its two northern and eastern sides facing inundations, and the southern flanked by a canal – was held by 421st and 429th Infantry Brigades. The higher points in the flooded area to the north were held by 422nd Infantry Brigade – which was little more than a screen. The area to the south was covered by 23rd, 45th and 47th Infantry Brigades, the 501st Infantry Brigade held the Duaiji line in the rear, while 81st Infantry Brigade was in reserve together with a tank battalion and the corps- and divisional commando battalions. The division was supported by 32 artillery batteries, comprising 190 tubes, and some 50 MBTs, while air defence was provided by four light gun batteries and two 'Grail' platoons.[31]

Further south, on the Faw Peninsula, Maher's VII Corps sill had

A group of Iraqi soldiers with suitably-decorated OT-62, as seen during the later stages of what they termed 'al-Hassad al-Akbar'. (via Ted Hooton)

A scene from one of several bridgeheads established by the Pasdaran on the western side of the Fish Lake on 9 and 10 January 1987. (Albert Grandolini Collection)

1 IRAN'S LAST CHANCE

An IRIAA AH-1J Cobra, armed with rocket launchers, passing above Iranian position in Shalamcheh region, during Operation Karbala-5. (Farzin Nadimi Collection)

An Iraqi BMP-1 captured by the IRGC during the opening blows of the Operation Karbala-5. (Photo by S. E.)

This MT-LB APC was also captured by the troops of one of the IRGC's naval brigades, and instantly deployed against its former owners. (Photo by S. E.)

Burned hulks of military trucks and smashed buildings were all that was left of the Iraqi military base in Duiji. (Photo by S. E.)

the 15th Infantry Division on the bank opposite Abadan, and could enfilade the attackers with some 160 guns as well as multiple rocket launcher systems (MRLS).

The primary Iraqi problem was neither the lack of troops, nor that of fire-power – but complacency. After successfully defeating Karbala-4, the defenders convinced themselves that they had substantially weakened the enemy. With generous leave policies still in place many units were under strength. To compensate, brigade commanders reduced the strength of their forward units, while some reserves were not alert. These problems were known not only to the Iranians but also to Saddam's Jordanian friend, King Hussein, who flew to Baghdad to warn Saddam. The Iraqis, who anticipated only raiding parties, appear to have ignored these warnings, although fear of raiders made the defenders nervous on the night of 8-9 January 1987 as it began to rain. Correspondingly, they began firing flares in an attempt to detect enemy activity. It was these flares which detected the 'Imam Reza' Division forming up on Umm Rassas 30 minutes before H-Hour, and prompted its commander to order an immediate attack.

Martyrdom Junction

As some 50,000 Pasdaran advanced on a 25 kilometre front, the Iraqi outposts fell back. In the north, the Iranians waded or swam the inundated areas to outflank many of the smaller positions, and it appears there was little serious fighting beyond the Fish Lake. Early in the morning, the IRIAF flew 30 attack sorties: while these hit numerous Iraqi headquarters and significantly bolstered the morale of ground troops, they also alerted the enemy.

On the right flank of the Task Force Karbala, the IRGC's Imam Hossein and Sarallah Divisions landed on the western bank of the Fish Lake and secured part of the embankment covering the southern causeway. Troops from Sarallah then forced their way down the causeway to take the southern strong point by 05.00hrs in the morning. Engineers supporting them then got a single T-55 tank across the causeway – just in time to face the first counterattack launched by the 5th Mechanised Division, the 66th Special Forces Brigade and the 8th Mechanised Brigade of the 3rd Armoured Division. Acting as a mobile pillbox, this single T-55 was to provide the centrepiece of Iranian frontlines for the next two days. Manned by successively replaced crews – brought over the lake by Kashayar APCs, together with ammunition and fuel – it proved crucial in defeating several Iraqi counterattacks. The IrAF flew about two dozens of air strikes attempting to hit it, but to no effect: the muddy terrain absorbed the effects of ordnance that detonated, while dozens of bombs failed to explode at all. Before long, like a lethal garden, the area was dotted by dozens of unexploded bombs. The Iraqi artillery fire grew to such intensity, and caused so many casualties, that the place became known to Iranians as the 'Martyrdom Junction': even the wounded were reluctant to seek evacuation across the causeway.

Troops of one of the naval brigades of the IRGC inside the completely ruined village of Duiji, early during the Operation Karbala-5. (Photo by S. E.)

Ultimately, after reportedly firing more than 300 shells, the gun of the lonesome T-55 overheated to the point of blowing up, forcing the crew to evacuate the tank. Ironically, while not a single tanker was killed while using this vehicle, its last crew was martyred while trying to take cover outside the vehicle, by one of the rare bombs dropped by Iraqi fighter-bombers at Martyrdom Junction that did explode, two days into Karbala-5.[32]

Meanwhile, the Pentangle was struck from the north by the Seyed o-Shohada and Ali Ibn Abu-Talib Divisions from the Task Force Qods, and by the 'Ashura' Division of Task Force Najaf from the east. Fierce resistance forced the commitment of Qods' Ansar al-Hossein Division, while – despite an Iraqi counter-attack – the Seyed o-Shohada Division penetrated the Pentangle by 11.15hrs (and the Iraqis admitted this, latter the same day). Interestingly, Tehran subsequently claimed taking 287 prisoners of war on the first day, and 610 on the second day, of Karbala-5 – indicating that many other Iraqis escaped the onslaught.

Meanwhile, the 'Imam Reza' Division – supported by one mechanised brigade of the IRGC – led the envelopment by the Task Force Najaf along the Shalamcheh Salient, by striking southwards, while the 'Nasr' Division advanced westwards despite fierce resistance from the isolated 47th Infantry Brigade.

Iranian Tactics

During the Iran-Iraq War, and ever since, there was, and still is, much talk about so-called 'human wave' assaults by the Iranian military. While there is little doubt that such attacks were launched – spontaneously and at minor scale – by a few Iranian commanders for different reasons, time and again; in reality the IRGC's Pasdaran and Basiji units relied upon constant infiltration – or 'swarming' – by night for overcoming the massive fortifications of major Iraqi frontlines during this phase of the war. Indeed, according to multiple Iraqi officers interviewed over the time, it was the Iranian infantry and its tactics that they feared the most.

With these tactics, the Iranians sought to encircle enemy positions and then push 200 to 500 metres deep within and thus effect what they called the 'attack from within'. Once in such position, the Pasdaran would take strongpoints under fire with their heavy weapons – including anti-tank armament – 'drench' them with fire from automatic weapons, and thus isolate them before an assault by the Basiji. The latter generally showed strong disregard for any kind of tactical finesse and often expended their limited ammunition supply – in turn leaving themselves defenceless to Iraqi counter-attacks. By contrast, Pasdaran assaults succeeded much more often because their experienced junior officers and NCOs directed attacks upon each formation's well-defined objectives – even if uncertain of their next objective. Throughout the entire war, it was foremost the lack of entrenching tools and fire-support, as well as Iraqi artillery barrages and air strikes on Iranian communication lines that hampered their ability to consolidate positions they have reached.

Over the time, a pattern developed along which the Iranians would attack after dusk and spend most of the night reducing Iraqi centres of resistance, before the dawn brought the Iraqi response.

One of the embarkation points for IRGC units on the eastern side of the Fish Lake. (Albert Grandolini Collection)

A group of Pasdaran mopping up the recently captured Iraqi position, including an operational T-55, during Karbala-5. (Albert Grandolini Collection)

The Pasdaran cheering the crew of an AH-1J Cobra underway low over their positions along the embankment of the Fish Lake, on 5 January 1987. (Tom Cooper Collection)

Trading Hot Punches

From dawn of 10 January 1987, the Sarallah- and the newly-deployed Karbala and Mohammad Rasoolallah Divisions absorbed Iraqi counterattacks and then, during the evening, pressed forward through the Pentangle defences, collapsing the salient by the end of the day. This success was based on a major violation of Iraqi radio security noted not only by the Iraqi, but also by the Iranian intelligence.[34] The next day, the Iranians claimed to have taken 1,000 prisoners and that the survivors fell back upon the River Duaiji although 5th Mechanised Division (Major General Salah Aboud Mahmoud) launched counter-attacks to support the beleaguered infantry. Undertaken by the 25th Mechanised Brigade of the 6th Armoured Division and the 34th Armoured Brigade of the 1st Mechanised Division, this counter-stroke was channelled by muddy terrain to the bridges over the Duaiji, and thus easily held up by the Pasdaran that were abundantly supplied with light anti-armour weapons.

Left without a choice, the Iraqis – who remained in possession of aerial dominance over the front-lines – flew fierce air strikes on the concentration points behind the Iranian frontlines. Between 9 and 12 February, the IrAF flew 662 sorties, including about a dozen by Tu-22 bombers. These began deploying even Nassr-5 and Nassr-9 bombs – Iraqi copies of the Soviet-made FAB-5000 and FAB-9000 bombs. Furthermore, the IrAAC flew 433 helicopter sorties, the vast majority over the Basrah area. The Iranian fire-support remained weak and the GMID – which had largely assembled the enemy ORBAT by 12 January 1987 – noted that the Iranian artillery was restricted to an average of about 100 tubes firing no more than 5,000 rounds a day.[35]

Duri tried to stabilise the situation during the next two days using counter-attacks by Brigadier Salman Hamid Abbdullah's 3rd Armoured Division, aiming to contain the Task Force Karbala's bridgehead. However – and contrary to what the Iraqi propaganda claimed – he failed to drive the enemy into the Fish Lake and the 12th Armoured Brigade even lost its commander on 10 January. To prop up the southern front, Duri then brought in the 8th, 20th, 46th Mechanised and 65th Special Forces Brigades, the latter supporting 8th Division's counter-attacks on the Fish Lake bridgehead. However, IRIAA's AH-1s hit back with TOWs and claimed many armoured vehicles, despite the intensive activity of IrAAC's anti-armour teams composed of Mi-25s and either Hughes MD.500s or Aerospatiale SA.342 Gazelles.[36]

Duri thus proved unable to prevent the further Iranian build-up along the Duaiji, which brought the troop strength to about 65,000, but also enabled Iranian engineers to construct causeways across the inundated areas; these were used to bring in supplies, move some armour and re-deploy artillery. In the light of Iraqi air strikes, this proved a risky business – as witnessed by a group of journalists the

Starting at first light, the Iraqis would react with a rain of shells; air- and mortar-bombs, air- and ground-launched rockets; prior to launching their counterattacks while the Iranians were trying to hold captured positions. Provided enough of them survived, they would continue the process of eroding the defences the next night. Iranian artillery and mortar batteries were active in forcing Iraqi troops to run a gauntlet during daylight, and one Iraqi general later referred to the battle in early 1987 as 'The Somme of the Iran-Iraq War'.[33]

Many of the lighter bombs dropped by Iraqi fighter-bombers failed to detonate when hitting the muddy battlefields of Karbala-4 and Karbala-5. This French-made example was photographed during the latter operation. (Farzin Nadimi Collection)

As during Karbala-4, the IrAF deployed its Tu-22 bombers into strikes on major assembly points for Iranian troops involved in Karabla-5. Their primary armament consisted of such massive bombs as the FAB-5000 and FAB-9000, or their locally manufactured copies, Nassr-5 and Nassr-9. (Tom Cooper Collection)

One of the embarkation points for Pasdaran and Basiji units during the Operation Karbala-5. Whenever recognized by the Iraqi resistance, such areas were heavily bombed by the IrAF. (Photo by E. S.)

Iranians attempted to bring up to Shalamcheh. Nevertheless, the IRIA and the IRGC managed to concentrate their artillery on a relatively narrow, 5-kilometre front and during the night from 11 to 12 January they unleashed a hurricane of fire upon the defenders. When the barrages lifted the Pasdaran and Basiji swept forward in numbers and, acting upon improved tactical training, penetrated multiple Iraqi positions. The few strongpoints not overrun immediately were isolated and exposed to a combination of artillery- and machine-gun fire. Although the Iraqis did manage to disrupt this attack and then regain some positions with the sheer volume of their fire on the next day, the Iranians continued pumping men and material into the frontline and kept their momentum. By the morning of 12 January, the Iraqi 426th Brigade was forced back, thus turning the entire frontline of the 11th Division right. In this fashion, the Iranians opened a way forward along the highway from Basra to Khorramshahr.[37]

Meanwhile, the advance of Najaf's 'Imam Reza' Division along Twaila Island was slow and bloody but the Iranians secured this piece of real estate by the same morning.[38] A force of some 3,000 from the Nasr Division then crossed the Shatt near the wrecked Abu al-Khasib refinery on 12 January. This bridgehead was contained by the 76th Infantry- and 68th Special Forces Brigades from the 15th Division, and driven out by 14 January – with help of a heliborne landing on the islands.[39]

At the AFGC, the Chief-of-Staff Lieutenant-General Abd al-Jawad Dhanoon (also 'Dhannan/Thanoon/Zanun') was being urged by his Operations Chief, Major-General Nizar Abdel Karim al-Khazraji, to use III Corps' reserve (including the 3rd Armoured and 5th Mechanised Divisions), and 10th Armoured Division to stage a counter-offensive sweeping down from north of the Fish Lake to roll up the enemy. Dhanoon dithered, partly because it would mean seeking Saddam's permission to commit the armour, and partly because Duri had committed much of his armoured reserve piecemeal and was unable to extract it. At best the corps commander was mediocre and ignored advice, never tried to anticipate the enemy and always reacted to Iranian attacks. His command style was to shout down radios and telephones threatening death and damnation if his bewildered subordinates did not immediately resolve the latest crisis. The constant deployment and rotation of brigades aggravated the situation, for with some 100 brigade movements during Karbala-5, junior commanders had no time to familiarize themselves with the situation before they entered the line and many became casualties while personally trying to find out what was going on.[40] (39).

During 12 January, Defence Minister Adnan Khairallah Talfah inspected the battlefield and ordered the Medina Manarwah Armoured Division of the Republican Guards – which was still undergoing training – to be sent south, indicating the fate of the offensive would now be determined by the size of reinforcements each side could bring up.[41] Success was also determined by the logistical organisation, and in this regard the more experienced staff of the Iraqi Army and well-maintained supply links proved more successful. However, the concentrated Iranian artillery fire – estimated with exaggeration by one Iraqi at 5,000 barrels –

A photo of the Iraqi-made Nassr-9 – a copy of the FAB-9000, which the Iraqis calculated packed about 60% of its original's punch – as it used to be posted in front of the IrAF HQ in Baghdad. (via Ali Tobchi)

proved daunting even for experienced troops and left many shell-shocked.[42] Furthermore, Khairallah authorized the use of chemical weapons. However, with the two sides closely entangled they could be deployed only against the enemy communications and supply dumps: these were subjected to repeated airborne mustard gas strikes. One Iranian survivor noted he never encountered fighting as ferocious as that in Karbala-5 and added: "I really did not want to fight'.[43]

Indeed, the sheer exhaustion of combatants on both sides resulted in a decline in fighting between 13 and 16 January. Nevertheless, the Imam Reza and Shohada Divisions – reinforced by multiple Basiji battalions – made another push. They forced the 45th and 478th Brigades to withdraw and secured the headquarters of the Duaiji sector. Encouraged, the Iranians committed their reserves from the Task Force Nooh and deployed the Abolfazl al-Abbas Infantry- and Qa'em-e-Mohammad Mechanised Divisions, together with the Nabi al-Akram Infantry- and Khatam al-Anhiya Artillery Brigades without success. By that time, casualties were so heavy that already on 13 January 1987, the Ministry of the IRGC called upon citizens to register for the 'Division of the Prophet Mohammed' in hope of raising 500,000 men from mosques, factories and offices. Eventually, even Tehran had to admit that only 200,000 followed the call – and that was probably an overestimate. As the appeal was issued Rafsanjani visited the forward battle headquarters and encouraged further efforts, but by 11 February all of the divisions had been battered, with the IRGC alone losing 974 company-, battalion-, brigade- and divisional commanders.

Lethal Skies

The long nights and low cloud cover of mid-January and early February 1987 had provided at least some shelter from Iraqi air power. However, whenever the weather permitted, the IRAF was airborne. Between 13 and 17 January, its pilots and those of the IrAAC flew 1,600 and 1,289 sorties, respectively, most over the Basra front. The Iranians reacted with their integrated air defence system, which inclued MIM-23B I-HAWK SAM-sites deployed east of the Karoun River, and these claimed both a MiG-23 and a Tupolev Tu-16 bomber on the first day of the offensive (the latter while underway at 40,000ft/12,200 metres, and because a pair of Mirage F.1 fighter-bombers equipped with French-made Caiman pods for electronic countermeasures failed to appear).[44]

The presence of HAWKs – reinforced by clandestine US-deliveries of spares – restricted the Iraqi airpower over the battlefield, even more so because these were linked with Skyguard anti-aircraft artillery systems. The Iranians took some time to move their air defence system and eventually, by 13 February 1987, their ground troops were operating at the very edge of the same. This in turn exposed them not only to additional air strikes, but also to the full force of Iraqi attack helicopters. On the other side, in response to repeated – even if few in numbers – Iranian air strikes on their headquarters, the Iraqis felt forced to deploy at least one SA-2 SAM-site within the sector protected by the VII Corps.

Baghdad latter announced that during January and February 1987 its air force lost up to 50 combat aircraft – or 10% of its total strength – together with numerous experienced pilots. However, such a loss rate was never confirmed by official documentation, and has since been fiercely denied by all available Iraqi sources.[45]

The IRIAF had meanwhile increased its operational strength, but with less than 60 fully operational fighter-bombers, it was usually on the defensive. Held back for defence of critically important installations deeper inside Iran, its F-14s were not used for attack purposes and rarely approached the frontlines. Even more problematic was the status of the IRIAF's early warning radar network which, by this time in the war, was not only badly damaged by earlier fighting, but also in state of disrepair. Combined with extensive knowledge about this network provided to the Iraqis by Iranian defectors already before the war, and Tehran's failure to at least rebuild if not reinforce IRIAF's radar-equipped units, this resulted in the Iranians gradually losing the big picture of the situation over the frontlines.

On the contrary, bolstered by spares obtained during the Irangate affair, the IRIAA remained airborne over the battlefield and used BGM-71 TOW ATGMs as often as possible, keeping the Iraqi armour at bay. Indeed, the activity of Iranian Cobra attack helicopters was such that the Iraqis rushed to the frontlines shells equipped with anti-helicopter proximity fuses, which could match TOWs' 3.75km maximum range. At least according to Iraqi sources, such shells proved highly effective.[46]

Republican Guards to the Rescue

On 14 January 1987, the Pasdaran began pushing into the 11th Infantry Division's left flank through half-burned palm groves, slowly forcing it out of the Duaiji Line and into the Jasim Line. This was a brutal, frontal attack, leaving behind a ghastly trail of bodies – and body parts – along the berms crossed by Iranian troops. However, this success of the IRGC led to momentous changes the following day, when Saddam chaired a meeting of the AFGC attended by Defence Minister Khaiallah, Chief-of-Staff Dhanoon, his Operations Director Khazraji, III Corps' commander Duri, the Director of Military Planning General Mohammad Abdul Qader, and 11th Infantry Division's commander General Shannan al Rabat. Saddam demanded to know what had happened and received a vague response from Dhanoon. Khazraji was franker pointing out that he, Dhanoon and Qader had all been in III Corps' forward command post and seen that Duri was nervous, shouting and cursing. He said Duri failed to recognize the true situation and was confusing Shannan. Duri's response was confused and he accused Dhanoon of failing to assist him. The two were soon exchanging angry words whereupon Saddam and Khaiallah stormed out of the meeting. Saddam soon expressed his wrath with Dhanoon: he was retired on the spot and replaced by Lieutenant-General Saad ad-Din Aziz. Duri was ordered to exchange positions with the commander of V Corps, Dhiya ad-Din Jamal; while the Director of Operation Khazraji was given the command of I Corps. Finally, Commander

A still from a rare video showing an Iranian military bulldozer in the process of erecting one of a myriad of earthen berms used as primary combat positions by both sides on the southern frontlines of the Iran-Iraq War. (Tom Cooper Collection)

following morning and briefly held up the IRGC, even if failing to prevent them from taking the last strongpoints of the Duaiji Line.

On the contrary, after bringing in additional reinforcements, five divisions of the Task Force Qods – supported by three tank battalions – used this area as a springboard for their new attack towards the Jasim. Despite heroic resistance from 18th, 44th and 704th Brigades, the Iranians punched through, took 2,010 prisoners, and established a kilometre-deep bridgehead, on 19 January 1987.

The next day, the Seyed o-Shohada and Sarallah Divisions renewed this assault by attempting another break-through, but this time they were held by 18th, 83rd, 101st, 704th Infantry Brigades (controlled by the 8th Infantry Division), and the 10th Guards Armoured Brigade. While the Iranians retained their bridgeheads on the shores of the Fish Lake and the Shatt, the Iraqis meanwhile frantically threw up a new defensive position behind the Jasim line along the Zawji (Dual) Canals, which helped to feed the Fish Lake from the Shatt. The Guards were again committed and their counter-attacks helped to restrict enemy progress. In comparison, the Iranians made little attempt to fortify their hard-won ground although their engineers did build berms alongside the main roads to conceal their traffic from enemy artillery observers.

Behind the Jasim line there was hectic engineering activity directed by the Sandhurst-trained GCHQ Logistics Chief, Lieutenant General Salim Hussein. He ordered several flooded areas to be drained and the construction of additional berms and roads. Two berm-based defensive positions were built at 5 kilometre intervals behind the Jasim line with 'Baghdad' and 5th Mechanised Divisions manning the first, while 12th Armoured and 3rd Armoured Divisions manned the second, using these as the basis for counter-attacks. On 22 January 1987 there was a new assault upon the Jasim line where 2nd Infantry Division (Brigadier Ahmad Rakan) had been brought in to hold the northern section on the right of 5th Mechanised Division, while 32nd Infantry Division had been moved north from the Shatt to hold the southern section leaving 11th Infantry Division in the middle like the meat in a sandwich. Fresh units launched successive night attacks and by the afternoon of 23 January the Iranians claimed 2,235 prisoners.

After stopping the initial wave of Iraqi counter-attacks, the Iranians re-launched their offensive. Progress was painfully slow as the Iraqis resisted fiercely with the Pasdaran having to storm each position. Nevertheless, by 26 January 1987 Tehran claimed to have secured a bridgehead across the Zawji Canals and the Iraqi engineers were forced to quickly build another defensive belt behind the waterway. On the night of 27/28 January Task Force Qods tried to break-out of this bridgehead using the Sarallah Division while Task Force Karbala launched diversions with the Imam Hossain and Al-Mahdi Divisions, reinforced by Najaf-Ashraf Division from 'Nooh'. This time, the Iraqis contained the situation by the following

A grim scene from a shallow Iranian trench opposing the Jasim Line, in early 1987. (Tom Cooper Collection)

of IV Corps, Thabit Sultan at-Tikriti, was replaced by Mohammad Abdul Qader. However, instead of taking over, Qader did not go straight to his new headquarters, but remained assigned to his old command – 11th Division, where he created additional defences in the rear until the situation stabilized, and acted as advisor to Shannan, who focused upon containing the enemy.[47]

Meanwhile, the arrival of 47th and – probably – 48th Infantry Brigades boosted the 11th Infantry Division, while the 5th Mechanised Division shored up its right with 94th, 702nd, 703rd, and 706th Infantry Brigades, as well as the 37th Armoured Brigade (whose commander was killed on 15 January 1987). Similarly, the Baghdad Republican Guards Infantry Division – supported by the 2nd Republican Guards Armoured Brigade of the Medina Division – struck the Fish Lake bridgeheads together with 18th Infantry Brigade.

Iranian progress was already very slow by the time Saddam finally did visit the front, on 17 January 1987, but the Duaiji line had almost been lost. Correspondingly, he demanded the rest of 'Medina' together with 'Baghdad' to stage a counter-attack the following afternoon. The Guards tried to make their way forward along roads clogged with traffic and reached the front only around dusk, only to discover that nobody had a clear idea what was going on. Nevertheless, the counter-attack was launched early the

This group of Pasdaran wearing gas-masks was photographed while they were in the process of outflanking the Duaiji Line by moving through the palm groves. (Farzin Nadimi Collection)

Firing the Koksan gun resulted in powerful wave of overpressure, as illustrated by this image from 1987. (Tom Cooper Collection)

Crew of one of the North Korean-made, calibre 170 mm M1978 Koksan self-propelled guns deployed on the frontlines near Basra, in 1987. The vehicle was left as painted and marked on delivery – including its overall olive green colour livery and the Red Star insignia. (Tom Cooper Collection)

morning: indeed, 5th Mechanised Division and Baghdad, with 12th Armoured Brigade finally overran the enemy bridgehead on west bank of Fish Lake later that day. The fighting between 27 January and 1 February involved 1,554 IrAF and 995 IrAAC sorties and then a brief pause descended upon the battlefield allowing 'Medina' Division of the Republican Guards to be withdrawn.

By now the Iraqis had suffered some 10,000 casualties, indeed so heavy that on 21 January Saddam called for volunteers between the ages of 14 and 35, while university students and any of their physically-fit lecturers under the age of 35 were told to enrol as officer candidates. Yet the pressure was severe enough for Saddam Hussein to send additional Guards units, while Maher's VII Corps not only provided artillery support but also a division as a back-stop to III Corps' right. Eventually, some 50 Iraqi brigades, including eight Guards, became involved in the battle, and there were reports that the dead were being ferried back to Baghdad in disguised vehicles, or kept in cold storage to regulate their release to relatives, while trains carrying casualties were being unloaded short of Baghdad.[48].

The Iranians maintained the pressure but by the end of the month the offensive was clearly running out of steam due to supply problems and the Pasdaran's shortage of both heavy equipment and command skills to exploit their successes. They had secured a 10 kilometre bridgehead inside Iraq and were within 12 kilometres of Basra, indeed they could see the eastern suburbs – but were exhausted. However, Iran brought the city under artillery and missile fire which did force the Iraqis to evacuate much of the civilian population.

Final Attempt

On the night of 31 January to 1 February 1987, the Karbala Task Force made a last effort around the Zawji Canals. The Imam Hossain and al-Mahdi Divisions assaulted, and reportedly achieved their greatest success on, the frontline held by the Iraqi 11th Division, where the gun line was reached. Nevertheless, the attackers were eventually driven back from the canals in a hard-fought battle with heavy Pasdaran losses to air power: the Iraqis are known to have flown 492 fixed- and 345 rotary-wing sorties on 1 February 1987 alone.

With the Iranians shooting their bolt and forced to pause and lick their wounds, the fighting died down for nearly a fortnight, during which the Iraqi 2nd Infantry Division relieved the battered 11th. As soon as they were ready, they counter-attacked again, this time against the northern side of the Iranian salient, while the III Corps assaulted along the western side of the Fish Lake before turning south to the Jasim River. This enterprise began as a combined-arms operation, but its components quickly devolved into private battles as the infantry and armour became separated and struck out at diverging angles with inadequate artillery support. The Iraqis lumbered forward so slowly in frontal assaults that they were rapidly stopped, although the pressure was sufficient to force the Iranians to abandon their Fish Lake bridgehead by 2 February. The counter-attack regained some 20 square kilometres of territory to pinch out the enemy salient by 7 February. Furthermore, this operation strained the Iraqi army to breaking point because, '…the Iraqi high command reduced its reserves to such a low level that, had the Iranians achieved a major breakthrough, it would have found itself short of reserve forces to stop the enemy'.[49]

After seven weeks of bitter fighting the Iranians were still outside Basra in terrain consisting '…of marsh, flooded terrain, and date palms, most of which had been reduced to stumps'.[50] There was intense, but inconclusive, fighting until mid February, during which the Iraqis did not perform well while attempting to advance. On the contrary, their army was ever more reliant upon defensive fire, water barriers, and high-performance fixed-wing aircraft – operations of which were frequently hampered by bad weather. Indeed, some secondary positions were virtually abandoned, together with much equipment and ammunition, and this may be why a number of Iraqi officers were reportedly executed.[51] However, the Iranians remained confined to their bridgehead, which was, meanwhile,

A trail of destroyed equipment and wrecked vehicles, left behind by the Pasdaran in the aftermath of Karbala-5. (Albert Grandolini Collection)

barely a kilometre wide in some places.

There was one more, brief, flare-up after the Iranians belatedly brought down armour and artillery from the Sumar front. On the night from 22 to 23 February the Imam Hossain Division spearheaded an assault along the Basra-Khorramshahr highway hitting the 39th, 116th, 423rd and 435th Brigades of the 2nd Division and pushing them back by two kilometres. However, this assault then came under sustained artillery fire from the west and south which, together with counterattacks of the 5th Mechanised Division and aerial activity (including 304 fixed-wing and 234 helicopter sorties between 23-25 February), helped smother the attack. Even the commander of the Imam Hossain Division, Hajj Hoseyn Kharrazi, was killed, apparently by an RPG round.

Loss of Strategic Initiative

On 26 February 1987, Tehran officially ended Karbala-5. This was a decision which finally recognised Iran's failure to achieve its war objectives – regardless of the cost. Certainly enough, a new Iranian attack struck 2nd Infantry and 5th Mechanised Divisions on the night from 28 February to 1 March 1987, and broke through in several places. However, the Baghdad Infantry Division of the Republican Guards counter-attacked and restored the line within 12 hours. Another similar attempt launched during the night of 3 to 4 March against 2nd Infantry Division in heavy rain and high winds, went as deep as three kilometres before it was stopped on 11 March, when Iranian commander Ahmad Rakan was killed.

Tehran was, meanwhile, facing pressure from new Iraqi attacks upon its cities and was diplomatically isolated even by Moscow and Damascus.

Starting with 12 January 1987, the IrAF bombed 62 Iranian cities and towns in 42 days, reportedly killing more than 6,000 people. This led to retaliation with artillery barrages against Basra in late January, encouraging a further flight of the civilian population from the city. A journalist visitor in late April noted: 'Parts of Basra are now completely deserted; and there is widespread damage from Iranian shelling, with many buildings (damaged) either by direct hits or shattered by shrapnel. Basra no longer functions as a city and this clearly can be counted as a propaganda coup for the Iranians'.[52] To help relieve the pressure, III Corps' new commander, Lieutenant General Dhiya Ad-din Jamal, launched a counter-offensive around the Jasim River on 1 March. IrAF commander, Air Marshal Hamid Shaaban at-Takriti, meanwhile closely cooperated operations of his branch and this ensured aerial reconnaissance information that was swiftly passed down to field commanders. However, while regaining a third of the ground lost in Karbala-5, this counteroffensive also caused excessive losses.[53]

Meanwhile, Tehran proclaimed a triumph claiming to have taken nearly 2,900 prisoners, and captured 220 AFVs and 85 guns as well as 155 square kilometres. An indirect confirmation of the gains were repeated strikes by heavy artillery and, reportedly, MLRS upon Basra's suburbs. However, while theoretically gaining a

Wreckage of one of up to 30 IrAF aircraft (a Su-22M-3 in this case), shot down by Iranian air defences during Karbala-4 or Karbala-5. (Tom Cooper Collection)

Victorious Iraqis with captured Pasdaran following what Baghdad named 'The Great Harvest', in March 1987. (Albert Grandolini Collection)

springboard for a future assault upon the city, Karbala-5 was another Iranian defeat – at both operational and strategic levels. It was only in regards of internal policy that it provided a boost for Rafsanjani who had been smeared by his opponents over the Irangate affair which had been publicised over the past months.

The cost was heavy; it was estimated that the Iranians had suffered 52,000-62,000 casualties (including 17,000 dead) and, while this figure may be exaggerated, the slaughter of the Basij must have been especially severe. Many of those lost, especially on the Iranian side, were veterans and the Iranian authorities now faced great difficulties finding volunteers for the Pasdaran and Basiji with quotas allocated to regions, towns and ministries. The well of courage and dedication, even within these revolutionary shock troops, had been drained low and there was a reluctance in their ranks to make further attacks. This reflected declining national morale among the war-weary population at a time when declining oil revenues, ebbing cash reserves and arms embargoes were sapping the Iranian war machine. One commentator noted: "Undeniably, Iran sorely needs a vast influx of new weaponry, at the very least a sustained infusion of spares to mobilise its air force, artillery and armour. Despite huge amounts spent on the black market, and what it was able to squeeze out of President Ronald Reagan in clandestine shipments, Iran still has not been able to amass sufficient new hardware to exploit its tactical superiority."[54]

The Iraqis – who called this battle 'The Great Harvest' (al-Hassad al-Akbar'), lost over 40,000 troops (including about 6,000 dead), up to 30 aircraft, over 700 tanks and other armoured vehicles, 250 artillery pieces and 1,400 other vehicles. This was a high price, but they prevented an Iranian break-through and imposed upon their enemy the growing and demoralizing realisation that Iran lacks adequate material resources. Perhaps more importantly: while his forces had just about contained the threat, Saddam felt forced to encourage greater professionalism between his commanders, and raise the morale of his nation. When the Iranian New Year ('Norouz/Nowrouz/Nowruz') ended without a clear-cut victory on 20 March 1987, he organized mass demonstrations in Baghdad.

Unsurprisingly, this prompted commentary like 'the fact that his government regarded not being defeated as victory was a testimony to the static defence to which it had become wedded over the past five years'.[55] Somewhat unfairly, another foreign observer concluded 'Ultimately, Iraq's generals prevailed ... in spite of the forces under their command rather than because of them'.[56] On the contrary, the British Military Attaché in Baghdad, Aldridge, summed up 'The battle was large-scale, bloody, prolonged by local standards and horrendous in its casualties to both sides'.[57]

Operation 'Karbala-8'

Understanding the danger of losing the strategic initiative, in April 1987 Iran launched a series of minor offensives – Karbala-7, Karbala-9 and Karbala-10 – on the northern front, aiming to pin down potential Iraqi reinforcements, but also as a reprisal for air attacks. Furthermore, knowing the last offensive caused the draining of the flooded area between the Fish Lake and the border, while waiting for the ground to dry, the IRGC commenced preparations for one last push towards Basra – Operation Karbala-8. In order to expand the salient south of the Fish Lake and improve their tactical position – perhaps also to prepare a bigger jump-off point for the next offensive – the IRGC assembled about 46,000 fresh troops. Clearly, most of the involved divisions were still licking their wounds, and thus additional divisions were brought in, resulting in a concentration of 10 divisions and their following deployment:

- Task Force Karbala, some 45,000 strong, was to strike from the northern bridgehead on the Jasim, north-westwards across the Zawji Canals and then roll up the southern section of the Fish Lake defences to the lower causeway.[58]
- Task Force Qods, about 20,000 strong, was to strike down the causeway.

On the Iraqi side, 2nd Infantry Division had been relieved by the 8th, which now held the southern part of the Fish Lake, while 19th Infantry Division faced the northern face of the Iranian salient, with 32nd Infantry Division on its right and two brigades of 5th Mechanised Division in reserve. On 1 April GMID noted unusual vehicle movements in the southern zone from late March, while on 31 March two spies reported troops forming up for an attack. Nevertheless, knowing the enemy had suffered heavy casualties, the Iraqis were convinced the Iranians were left with only 60 artillery pieces and complacently failed to expect a major assault.[59] Thus, the Iraqis did nothing when hundreds of pick-up trucks were used to deploy Pasdaran and Basiji within 1.5 kilometres of their jump-off points, and then made their final approach on foot.

Ya Saheb az-Zaman!

The code-word Ya Saheb az-Zaman ('Oh Lord of the Era' or 'Hidden Imam') was issued during the night of 6 to 7 April 1987,

Table 3: Order of Battle for Operation Karbala-8, April 1987

Corps	Division	Brigades
Iran		
Task Force Karbala	8th Najaf Ashraf Division IRGC	
	10th Seyed o-Shohada Division IRGC	
	17th Ali Ibn Abu-Talib Division IRGC	
	19th Fajr Division IRGC	
	25th Karbala Division IRGC	
	27th Mohammad Rasoolallah Division IRGC	
	31st Ashura Division IRGC	
	33rd al-Mahdi Division IRGC	
	83rd Ramadan Armoured Brigade IRGC	
Task Force Qods	21st Imam Reza Division IRGC	
	32nd Ansar al-Hossein Division IRGC	
	18th al-Ghadir Brigade IRGC	
Iraq		
III Corps	5th Mechanised Division	26th Armoured & 27th Mechanised Brigades
	8th Infantry Division	106th, 418th Infantry Brigades
	19th Infantry Division	44th, 417th Infantry Brigades
	32nd Infantry Division	29th, 41st, 73rd, 117th, 441st Infantry Brigades
Reinforcements	Hammurabi Armoured Division Republican Guards	8th & 17th Armoured, 15th Mechanised Brigades Republican Guards
	Medina Manarwah Armoured Division Republican Guards	2nd & 10th Armoured, 14th Mechanised Brigade Republican Guards
	Baghdad Infantry Division Republican Guards	4th, 5th, 6th, 7th Infantry Brigades Republican Guards

and troops of the Task Force Qods launched their assault. Almost instantly, they established bridgeheads around the southern causeway with two battalions each of the Imam Reza Division and al-Ghadir Brigade, but these were unable to continue their advance due to intense artillery fire.[60] Similarly, Task Force Karbala's attack with 10 battalions was pinned down for two hours by prompt artillery fire and before it could hit positions of the 19th and 32nd Divisions, even if not before the Pasdaran forced their way into two of former's strongpoints.

On 10 April, Karbala attempted to exploit its penetration through deployment of 30 battalions, supported by a battalion of MBTs and APCs each from the IRIA's 81st Armoured Division, and about 70 artillery pieces. Simultaneously, Task Force Qods renewed its attempts to force the causeway through 8th Infantry Division. However, in all of these cases, the hard-won gains were swiftly obliterated by armour-lead counter-attacks launched with strong air support. The IrAF flew over 300 fixed-wing sorties and the IrAAC another 206 by helicopters on 8 and 9 April, deploying chemical weapons in abundance. The IRIAA appeared only occasionally, while the IRIAF held itself back. Correspondingly, the only available means of air defence were a few batteries of ZSU-23-4 Shilka self-propelled guns, and about a dozen MANPAD-teams equipped with SA-7s. Unsurprisingly, the Iranians found themselves exposed to continuous counterattacks and one Pasdaran later commented:

It was just like we were sitting near an airport and airplanes easily approached and calmly dropped their loads along with leaflets telling us to go back to our homes.[61]

Like so many times before, the conclusion was unavoidable, that the IRGC-officers were the architects of their own misfortune: they rarely – if ever – co-ordinated operations with the IRIAF and even when Grumman F-14A Tomcat fighters were flying combat air patrols 20-30 kilometres behind the frontlines, would not call upon them to help. Such failures were a result of a combination of factors, including pride, shortage of VHF radios, and the fact the Pasdaran were often not sure of their exact location. Indeed, not a few supply columns were destroyed because they were sent in wrong direction.[62]

Ultimately, assaults of Karbala-8 were broken off after a gain of only a kilometre in three days of fighting. Nevertheless the Iraqis were getting anxious. Just after midnight on 9 April 1987, the Soviet Military Attaché sought a special meeting with Iraqi military leaders to forward information from Moscow that at least four Pasdaran divisions and several brigades had received boats, bridges and other crossing equipment, which might suggest that Karbala-8 involved not just a crossing of the Fish Lake but also attacks either in the Hawizah Marshes or across the Shatt al-Arab.[63] For Baghdad it was vital to nip the offensive in the bud. On 11 April, a crushing response was unleashed in form of three divisions of the Republican Guards and 10 brigades of the army: Ibrahim Abdel-Sattar Muhammad's Hammurabi Republican Guards Armoured

Division, Ahmad Ibrahim Hammash's Medina Republican Guards Armoured Division and Kamil Sajit Aziz's Baghdad Republican Guards Infantry Division. Provided with overwhelming air- and artillery support they restored the situation to that before the last Iranian attack by the noon. They not only took many prisoners but also dashed all of Tehran's hopes of success. Certainly enough, the IRGC did receive some support from IRIAA's Cobras this time: these flew over 50 combat sorties. Similarly, the IRIAF fighter bombers hit several of Iraqi headquarters and communication facilities. But, that was not enough. The IrAF flew over 350 sorties in support of ground troops, and successfully interdicted Iranian communications between Shalamcheh and Khorramshahr. While suffering some 2,000 casualties, the Iraqis thus held the enemy 15 kilometres short of Basra, and boxed them into a salient exposed to artillery fire from three directions. In turn, while suffering some 6,500 casualties – or about 10% of the assault force – the Iranians failed not only to develop a viable springboard to Basra, but were left in realisation that no further advance was possible.[64]

Post Scriptum

Karbala-8 brought total Iranian casualties since late December 1986 to more than 85,000 and forced even the biggest hawks in Tehran to finally accept the reality: Iran lacked the material resources to end the war with a conventional blow. In despair, Rezai wrote a letter of resignation to Khomeini in April 1987, blaming – amongst other reasons – the lack of national support for the war effort. The Ayatollah refused his request: Rezai remained in his position until August 1997 when the Government accepted his second resignation letter.

Grudgingly, the religious-political leadership in Tehran admitted that the IRIA's generals had been right all along with their doubts about the country's ability to take Basra. In turn, the regular military overplayed its hand when demanding of religious-political leaders and the IRGC to recognize the fact that the impasse with Iraq could only be resolved through the means of diplomacy. This was something absolutely unacceptable for the clerics and their supporters, both of whom desperately insisted on a military solution. Eventually, a solution was found in emphasising the northern frontlines, and thus buying time until the situation in the south would be favourable enough to renew the assault upon Basra. It was a massive gamble based on assumptions that the Iraqis would remain as passive as they had acted the last five years. While appearing rational, it made no allowance for any changes in Saddam's strategy. Correspondingly, and before soon, a steady stream of IRGC's divisions began flowing northward.[65]

Rezai re-appeared in late June 1987, to reveal this new strategy with remarks that the Basra-offensives had 'put the war's decisive stage behind it… and (the war) has now entered a stage to determine the future of Iraq… (The coming struggle will be) a series of limited operations and a series of bigger ones. We have plans to organise, train and arm popular forces inside Iraq…This is the new front'.

Essentially, and years too late, Tehran decided to start supporting opposition to Saddam inside Iraq, notable the Kurds, in an attempt to weaken and destabilize the regime, erode and disperse its military strength – before renewing major attacks.[66]

In Baghdad, commanders around Saddam had already decided that only offensive operations would bring a favourable conclusion to the war. Even then – and as insurance against a new thrust around the Hawizah Marshes – they added another 32 kilometres of fortifications to extend the existing 88-kilometre line to cover Amarah.[67] On 5 March 1987, Saddam had held a top level meeting

The Iraqi Air Force dominated the skies over the battlefield during Karbala-5. This MiG-23BN was photographed while rushing very low above Iranian positions. (Farzin Nadimi Collection)

A grim scene from one of battlefields of Iranian Karbala offensives, showing dozens of bodies of the Pasdaran, probably killed by Iraqi chemical weapons. Although nearly breaking the back of the Iraqi army, ultimately, these operations destroyed the offensive power of the IRGC. (via Tom Cooper)

lasting five hours in Baghdad. Those attending included the Defence Minister Khairallah, a senior member of the Ba'ath Party Ali Hassan Al Mejid, and Information Minister Latif Nasif Jassem. The meeting reportedly considered strategy and raised concerns about the future for Iraq in a war of attrition. It decided to meet this situation by expanding the Republican Guard, escalating the Tanker War, and making even more extensive use of weapons of mass destruction.[68]

Notes for Chapter 1
1 CIA-RDP86T01017R000202020001-4.
2 Ibid.
3 CIA-RDP90R00961R000300060001-1.
4 CIA-RDP86T01017R000808180001-5.
5 For planning see Cordesman, *The Iran-Iraq War* pp.105, 123, hereafter Cordesman; Farrokh, *Iran at War* p.392, (hereafter Farrokh); Cordsman & Wagner, The Lessons of Modern War pp.245-246, hereafter Lessons; Malovany, *Milhamot Bavel ha-Hadasha* p.345, (hereafter Malovany); O'Ballance, *The Gulf War* pp.189-190 (hereafter O'Ballance); Pollack, Arabs at War p. 221 (hereafter. Pollack); Pollack, *The Persian Puzzle*, p.221, (hereafter Pollack, Puzzle); Zabih, The Iranian military in Revolution and War pp.194-195, hereafter Zabih. SH-GMID-D-000-301
6 Bulloch & Miller p.157.
7 For the defences see Bulloch & Miller p.157; Hiro, The Longest

War pp.180-181, (hereafter Hiro); Lessons p.149; National Training Center, The Iraqi Army: Organization and Tactics pp. 150, 153-154, hereafter NTC; Pollack pp. 203-204. Colonel B. Aldridge's Report para 52; US AISC p. 6-15; DIA DDB-2680-103-88 p.12; Edgar O'Ballance's article 'Iran vs Iraq: Quantity vs Quality?'; Richard Philipps article Tactical Defensive Doctrine of the Iraqi Ground Forces. Virtualglobetrotting web site 'Abandoned fortifications of the Iran-Iraq War.' The original version of this site, with images taken circa 1990 clearly showed the triangular strong points but they are almost obliterated in the more recent version whose images were taken some 20 years later.

8 Iraq deployed 4 million mines during the war with Iran and had some 6 million in stock. Mines were usually laid manually but the Iraqi Army also had Russian PMR-3 and Italian Valsalla minelayers, while many MLRS had rockets which could carry anti-personnel mines. The mines were acquired from Chile, China, Egypt, Italy, Singapore and the Soviet Union.

9 During the war shell fire destroyed millions of date palms while many more were lost to post-war salination.

10 For Coalition operations against Iraqi fortifications see Robert H.Scales' *Certain Victory*, pp.200-206, 226

11 Farrokh p.392; Pollack, Puzzle, p.221.

12 Cordesman, The Iran-Iraq War p. 123, hereafter Cordesman.

13 Buchan, Days of God p.369, hereafter Buchan.

14 For Karbala-4 see Cooper & Bishop *Iran-Iraq War in the Air*, pp.231-233 (hereafter Cooper & Bishop); Cordsman pp 103, 105, 109, 122-4; Farrokh pp.392-393; Hiro p 180; Lessons pp 245-247; Malovany pp.345-349; O'Ballance pp 189-192; Pelletiere, The Iran-Iraq War p.118 (hereafter Pelletiere); Pollack p. 221 passim; Ward, Immortal pp 277-278 hereafter Ward; Zabih pp.195-196, 242.

15 Cooper & Bishop p.232.

16 SH-GMID-D-000-301.

17 Brigadier-General Ahmad Sadik (retired officer of the Iraqi Air Force Intelligence Department), interview with Tom Cooper, March 2005

18 Rashid was described as 'colourful' by Nick Childs, 'The Gulf War: Iraq under pressure', *Jane's Defence Weekly*, 9 May 1987 pp.899-901, (hereafter Childs JDW)

19 'Return of 175 Iranian bodies from Iraq stirs painful memories', *al-Monitor*, 21 May 2015

20 After the war, both Iraqi corps commanders were accused of exaggerating enemy casualties to enhance their own prestige; see General Hamdani in 'Institute for Defense Analyses Project 1946', pp. 114-115 (hereafter Project 1946)

21 Murray & Woods p.293 & Buchan p.369

22 According to Zabih p.196 the new offensive, 'Karbala-5', had its origins in an invitation by Khamenei in late 1985 to a specially convened group of retired IRIA officers to plan an offensive against Basra

23 There was intermittent rain and fog from 19 December 1986 onwards, see Kuwait daily weather forecast provided by Freemeteo web site & Buchan p.369

24 Cordesman, The Iran-Iraq War and Western Security p.37, (hereafter Cordesman, Security)

25 For 'Karbala-5' see Al-Marashi & Salama *Iraq's Armed Forces* pp. 169-170 (hereafter Marashi & Salama); Cooper & Bishop pp.235-240. Cordsman p 125-131, 135-136. Farrokh pp. 393-395; Griffin, *The Iraqi Way of War*, pp.23-25 (hereafter Griffin); Hiro p 180-185. Lessons pp. 247-254, 269 f/n 101, f/n 104, f/n 114, 115, 116; Parviz Mosalla-Nejad, Shalamcheh pp. 30-55 (hereafter Mosalla-Nejad); O'Ballance p 195-198; Pelletierre pp.117-122; Pollack pp.221-224; Ward pp. 278-279; Project 1946 pp.114-118 (including an interview with General Raad Hamdani); Zabih pp. 196-199, 242-243; 'Imposed War Official Webite'sajed.ir (Karbala-5 entry); Colonel B. Aldridge's report Pars 52-53 & SH-GMID-D-000-266; SH-GMID-D-000-301.

26 Mosalla-Nejad p.33.

27 Ibid, pp.30-31.

28 While the IRGC's units generally operated a miscellany of APCs captured from the Iraqis, and some of Chinese and North Korean origin, they also deployed BTR-50s re-engined with US-made Diesels.

29 Four of the involved helicopters were used for supporting chemical decontamination operations. During Karbala-5 the IRIAA is known to have moved 5,292 troops with 108 tonnes of supplies and evacuated 5,601 injured.

30 Op-cit p.35. 'Ya Zahra' is a Shi'a chant popular with the IRGC, calling on Mohammad's fourth daughter, Fatemeh Zahra, for strength and perseverance.

31 Iraqi artillery was organized into battalions, designated 'regiments' – each consisting of three batteries.

32 P. P., veteran of Ramadan Armoured Brigade, IRGC, interview by Tom Cooper, December 2003 & A. R., former Iranian Army NCO, interview by Tom Cooper, February 2004

33 General Hamdani in *Project 1946* pp.114-118. The text describes him visiting the headquarters of 'V Corps' – although this was the headquarters of the 5th Mechanised Division.

34 SH-GMID-D-000-301. While some Iraqi sources remain sceptical about such reports, Iranian and other Iraqi sources cite that the two (E)C-130H Khoofash ('Bat') ELINT/SIGINT-aircraft operated by the IRIAF were capable of reading Iraqi radio communications in real time. For example, Brigadier-General Sadik (interview with Tom Cooper, March 2005), stressed that this was the reason why the IrAF repeatedly attempted to intercept such aircraft – although these operated relatively deep inside the Iranian airspace. Indeed, IrAF's pilots eventually claimed two of what the Iraqis believed would have been four (E)C-130Hs during the war. However, the IRIAF actually had only two such aircraft, and both are still operational as of 2017.

35 Sadik, interview by Tom Cooper, March 2005 & SH-GMID-D-000-301.

36 A. R. noted that during Karbala-5 the IRIAA's Cobras launched 67 TOW and claimed 43 AFVs.

37 NTC p.123

38 General Nawfal Ismail Khudayyir (Khudayyir), the 8th Inf Division commander, distinguished himself during Karbala-5 by retaking the island and was rewarded with command of 6th Armoured Division, which would take part in the 1988 Faw Peninsula offensive.

39 Cooper & Bishop p.237.

40 Aldridge *Report Para 53*.

41 *Lessons* p.251. Most accounts claim Saddam visited the front, but Malovany makes it clear it was Khairallah who kept a watching brief on III Corps.

42 Murray & Wood, *The Iran-Iraq War* p.294 (hereafter Murray & Wood), quoting memoirs of General Saadoun Hamdani & Malovany, p.354. The latter is providing a figure of 3,000, but most likely number of cases was about 1,700.

43 Mosalla-Nejad p.51.

44 According to Sadik (interview with Tom Cooper, March 2005), all sorties of IrAF's Tu-16 and Tu-22 bombers were supported by

an entire 'electronic warfare package' involving a pair of Mirage F.1EQ with Caiman ECM pods, others armed with Baz-AR anti-radar missiles, and Sukhoi Su-22s armed with Soviet-made AS-8 Kyle anti-radar missiles. However, on this occasion the Mirage failed to appear due to a combination of technical snags and bad weather, leaving one of the Tu-16-formations fatally exposed. Notable is that the Baz ('Falcon')-AR (AR stood for 'anti-radar') was a custom tailored version of the Anglo-French Martel missile with a more sophisticated, French-designed seeker head.

45 For example, Brigadier-General Sadik (interview with Tom Cooper, March 2005), strictly denied the possibility of the IrAF losing more than 23 aircraft during Karbala-5, and listed most of losses in question. A cross-examination with other (including Iranian) sources confirmed nearly all of his list, while providing details of only 2-3 additional losses of IrAF's combat aircraft during this period.
46 Sadik, interview with Tom Cooper, March 2005
47 General Makki, interview with Ted Hooton, March 2017. Contrary to certain other claims, 'Salahaddin' – Saad ad-Din Aziz – was not a Basra-born Shia but a Mosul-born Sunni. The changes of command were first reported in an Iranian communiqué of 25 February 1987, while the first public reference to Jamal commanding III Corps was an Iraqi Iraqi communiqué from 1 March 1987.
48 Childs JDW.
49 Hiro p. 182.
50 Lessons p. 253.
51 Al-Marashi and Salama p.169.
52 Childs JDW.
53 Al-Marashi and Salama p.169.
54 James Bruce, in Jane's Defence Weekly, 21 February 1987. Hereafter Bruce JDW
55 Hiro p 185.
56 Pollack p.224.
57 Aldridge report Para 48
58 After Karbala-5, the Ramadan Brigade had replaced its BTR-50s for M113s taken from the 16th Armoured Division IRIA.
59 SH-GMID-D-000-266. The Iranians were also supported by 34 helicopters, including 12 gunships which claimed almost 20 AFVs. However, the aircraft flew only 306 hours in five days.
60 For further details on Karbala-8 see Cooper & Bishop p.243; Cordsman p 139; Hiro p 185; Lessons pp. 260, 292- 3; Malovany pp. 360-362; Mosalla-Nejad pp.56-60; O'Ballance p 203; Zabih pp.199-200. SH-GMID-D-000-266.
61 P. P., veteran of Ramadan Armoured Brigade, IRGC, interview with Tom Cooper, December 2004
62 Ibid.
63 SH-GMID-D-000-266.
64 Ibid.
65 For the changes in Iraqi strategy, see Murray & Woods, p.320. Ironically, even at the end of 1987 the CIA continued to believe the next major Iranian attack would still be on the Southern Front. CIA-RDP90T00114R000700800002-2.
66 Lessons p.254, quoting Keyhan of 29 June and repeated in FBIS of 7 July 1987. We would like to thank Mr David Isby for his help in tracking this quote.
67 'Mobilisation problem for Iranian leaders', Jane's Defence Weekly, 2 April 1988, hereafter 'JDW, Mobilisation'.
68 Cordesman pp. 259-260.

2
TWO ARMIES

With the failure of 'Karbala-8' a year-long lull descended upon the southern battlefield – no doubt to the relief of the troops on both sides. But while there was some relief from danger there was none from discomfort. Therefore, the generals tried to ensure their men were never idle – for constant activity prevented them brooding.

During the day there were rear defences and roads to be both built and maintained as trucks brought men and supplies to the dumps at the rear; running the gauntlet of enemy artillery, heavy mortars, MLRS or roving helicopter gunships which targeted bottlenecks such as cross roads and the approaches to bridges. Safety from enemy fire was to be found in trenches and dugouts – with one Iraqi soldier recalling that as he went along the road all he could see was the heads of soldiers sticking out of the ground.[69] At the front both sides kept their heads down, with the daily monotony broken by the crack of a sniper's rifle aiming at the unwary, or the occasional harassing mortar bomb or shell. At night, seen through the green light of image intensifiers, the front resembled an ants nest. Supply convoys and replacements would file to the front line, whose garrisons would send forward work parties, ration carriers and reliefs to the advanced positions within the barbed wire and minefields. There, with every sense alert to raiders, the men spent the night laying mines, repairing or extending barbed wire entanglements, against a background of harassing fire which might suddenly concentrate upon tracks, bottlenecks or areas where the enemy knew, or suspected, there would be work parties. In the morning came the mournful task of counting and evacuating the casualties to hospital, or to the grave, and accounting for material losses.[70]

Both sides would stand-to before dawn and once the men had been stood down, around 05:00 in summer, they would have morning prayers. Daily prayers were the norm for both sides, but the Iraqi Army avoided formal Friday prayers although there was nothing to stop men using civilian mosques.[71].

Then came breakfast which, for Iranian troops, usually consisted of sweet tea, feta cheese and flat bread, very occasionally accompanied with scrambled eggs; while Iraqi troops would have cheese, milk, tea or soup cooked by squads in the front line, augmented by dates and onions. Lunch would be between noon and 13:00 although, for Iranian troops, it depended upon how well-supplied they were, or where they were fighting. If a hot meal was available it was cooked rice with lentils, or stews. A good treat was rice with chicken or cooked meat. Where they were unable to get a hot meal they used canned food, of which the most sought-after was tuna in oil. Dinner was around 20:00 to 21:00 and often consisted of abgoosht (a meat stew with chickpeas and beans), or thick Persian soups, but during the summer men settled for watermelon or grapes with feta cheese and bread.

The Iraqis tried to organize hot meals for both lunch and dinner.

The crew of an IRIA-operated Chieftain seen with their vehicle later during the war. Because of heavy attrition during earlier operations, but also of increased rivalry with the IRGC, they saw ever less action in 1986 and 1987. (via S. S.)

To shield themselves and their equipment from the summer heat, the crew of this IRIA-operated ZSU-23-4 improvised a sun shield atop the turret of their vehicle. (via E. S.)

This was cooked at the front whenever and wherever possible, but sometimes combat operations forced the meals to be merged. They consisted of rice, cooked vegetables with tomato sauce, and meat which was either beef or mutton – although twice a week this was replaced by chicken. Lunch was often augmented with dates or onions, while all meals included fruit depending upon the season. The men also received date syrup (dibis) or sesame syrup (rashi) during winter or on cold days to raise calorie levels. All meals were accompanied by universally-loved brown Army Bread baked in military bakeries from high-quality whole-wheat flour. This was famous for its unique taste and texture. Where the front line was some distance away it was cooked in mobile field kitchens, one per company, and then driven to the units on the frontline in insulated containers. Where intense combat was anticipated each unit would receive a week's supply of dry food.

Keeping this food edible, and equipment serviceable, was always a problem – regardless if in winter or in summer. The winter mist and rain forced men to repeatedly oil their weapons, but ammunition was often ruined, and the Pasdaran had problems with their telephone cables. Flooding created soft, clinging mud which could enter mess tins and give food a gritty taste. It slowed movement by foot or vehicle and worked its way into the operating rooms in the forward casualty posts and field hospitals. There were similar problems during the summer when the sun baked the ground so that vehicles or groups of men created plumes of dust which attracted the unwelcome attention of artillery observers. Sandstorms from north-westerly winds created drifts on the roads and could rapidly fill a trench while the men had to clean their weapons twice a day despite wrapping them in cloth.[72]

Heat, humidity and dust all affected the men and hardware to a greater or lesser extent. Indeed, during the summer the heat around noon could distort the gun barrels of MBTs. Therefore, and unless urgently required, all combat activity tended to take place before 10 o'clock in the morning and after 3 o'clock in the afternoon. Dust was the most serious problem, especially for electronic equipment (such as radios); although the Russian practice of using rotas to exchange

Due to lack of replacement equipment, but also poor quality of arms hurriedly acquired from China and North Korea, the Iranians were forced to make extensive use of armament captured from the Iraqis. This photograph came into being during the testing of French-made Milan ATGMs. (via E. S.)

modules eased the problem for Iraqi troops – while increasing demand in the supply system. Radio communication was affected by static electricity caused by dry air and sand storms effecting FM communications in the day and AM communications after midnight. A problem for AFV crews of both sides was that Russian and Chinese vehicles were designed for Arctic-like conditions and closed-down crews frequently suffered heatstroke.[73]

After more than six years of bloody fightingthe two armies, especially the Iranian, had changed significantly since September 1980.[74] Tehran's policy was summed up by the chant 'Jang, jang ba pirouzi' ('War, war until victory'), with which Pasdaran, Basiji and even Iraqi PoWs greeted Rafsanjani as he mounted the podium at the Tehran University Friday Sermon (formerly football) ground, on 4 July 1988, knowing the war was already lost.[75]

The Iranian Forces

Tehran's command structure remained very much the same as of 1982, with Khomeini the ultimate decision maker and nominal head of the SDC, whose members included the President Khamenei, and Premier Mir Hossein Moussavi together with the Defence Minister. Military personnel included Colonel Hussein Jalili and Revolutionary Guards Minister Mohsen Rafighdust, as well as the Ayatollah's professional representative on the council, Brigadier Zahirnejhad. The service chiefs included Armed Forces Chief-of-Staff, Colonel Sohrabi, IRIA commander Shirazi, and the Ground Forces Commander Colonel Hussein Hassani-Sa'di, the Pasdaran leader Mohsen Rezai and his Deputy Ali Shamkhani, together with the Air Force and Naval commanders. In May 1987 Khomeini promoted 10 senior officers for outstanding wartime service, with Zahirnejhad becoming a Major General, while Sohrabi, Shirazi, and Hassani-Sa'di , together with IRIAF commander Colonel Mansour Sattari becoming Brigadiers.[76]

The SDC was supported by a Joint Staff, drawn from the conventional and unconventional forces augmented by the National Police and the Gendarmerie, responsible for military planning and co-operation and operational control of all forces. It was based upon the US system with Personnel and Administration (J1), Intelligence and Security (J2), Operations and Training (J3), Logistics and Support (J4), Liaison (J5). The executive arm of the SDC was the Headquarters Western Operational Area, organised on similar lines to the Joint Staff but with Gendarmerie and National Police representatives. To ensure political reliability there was an SDC representative – usually the senior Pasdaran commander, together with Khomenei's personal representative. Decisions made by the SDC were executed through task force headquarters by the operations headquarters (OHQ) of which three faced the Iraqis; Northwest (NWOHQ) at Urumiyeh (or Urmia), West (WOHQ) at Kermanshah and South (SOHQ) at Ahvaz. These three were also known as Ramadan, Hamzeh Seyyed ash Shohada and Karbala, respectively.

Furthermore, there was Headquarters East Operational Area at Torbat-e Heydariyeh to secure the eastern frontier. These were usually IRIA/Pasdaran commands but the northern ones also had a strong police/gendarme presence. They were subdivided into 3-8 sectors whose operations might be co-ordinated by permanent task force headquarters.

It has been estimated that by 1987 out of 9 million men aged 18-45, Iran had 1.28 million in uniform.[77]

Although the IRIA, administered and supported by the Defence Ministry, had lost much prestige since the Iranian Revolution, especially among the politicians, it remained a formidable force which had been steadily expanded. The basic structure remained based upon the 16th, 81st and 92nd Armoured Divisions, and 21st, 28th, 64th and 77th (Mechanised) Infantry Divisions. Between 1981 and 1982 the 88th Armoured Brigade, the 30th, 58th and 84th Infantry Brigades were expanded into divisions followed in 1983 by the 23rd Special Forces Brigade, but the 37th Armoured, 40th Infantry and 55th Airborne Brigades were unchanged and a 45th Special Forces Brigade was created. This gave the IRIA 45 brigades, including 16 armoured/mechanised, 24 infantry and five special forces/airborne brigades. The majority of these were deployed with 11 divisions on the northern and central fronts.

Many of these units were filled out with temporary reservist or 'Qods' battalions, usually two or three at a time, with the 84th Brigade reported to have created a total of 20 such units during the war. The IRIA, whose strength was estimated by US Intelligence in July 1987 as 243,000-279,000, also provided a broad range of specialist services including the five pre-war artillery groups (11th, 22nd, 33rd, 44th, and 55th) – each of six or seven battalions – and engineer battalions.[78]

Depending on the task in question, the IRIAA usually forward-deployed one of its five aviation groups – 1st (Kermanshah), 2nd (Masjed-Soleiman), 3rd (Kerman), 4th (Esfahan), and 5th (Ghale-Morghi) – to major headquarters. Each was usually organized into one attack-, one or two assault- and one battalion of support aviation. The down-side of the IRIA's expertise was its reliance upon Western equipment – primarily American and British – for which the stream of spares had been dammed when the two governments damned Tehran for its diplomatic waywardness.

Inferior equipment from China and North Korea had to be used even by the IRIA which re-equipped three former Chieftain battalions – including the 293rd/3rd Brigade/ 92nd Armoured Division – with North Korean Chonma-ho Is, based upon the T-62. The quality of East Asian products was inferior to that of Soviet and Western manufacturers, Saddam being told during a meeting on 27 June 1988 of North Korean bombs detonating after being in the sun for only six hours. While Iraqis could afford the luxury of cancelling contracts for poor-quality of Chinese and North Korean ammunition, Iran could not: after all, China was estimated by US Intelligence to be providing 60-75% of Iran's arms requirements.[79]

Part of the IRIA and Pasdaran needs were met from the domestic military industry base established by the Shah, but by early 1987 Iran's whole industrial base was suffering steady erosion. Refining and electrical generation capacity were down by a third, although during the winter of 1986/1987 daily power cuts were reduced from up to seven hours a day to two.[80] Incompetence, but foremost endemic corruption with Ministry of the IRGC, meant that millions allocated for vital military production ended in private pockets: indeed most of the money allocated for domestic military production in 1987 was squandered or stolen and only the most minor projects were started. This was so successfully concealed that Rafsanjani learned of it only in the summer of 1988.[81]

Additional money had to be spent on the illicit trade in spares and equipment not only from the 'commercial' market but also from many of Uncle Sam's Asian allies, such as South Korea and Singapore, but also foes – like Vietnam. Even this was insufficient and the inventory of serviceable Western equipment slowly declined, the greatest problems being with artillery and helicopters; the former slowly wearing out to reduce battery strength by up to half, while the latter were most dependent upon scarce spares.

In part this explains why the IRIA was no longer the Iranian spearhead in favour of the Pasdaran and Basiji. The bemused professionals despaired of the slap-dash planning and preparation of the Pasdaran, but recognised their bravery. A former university student and conscript tank commander who served until October 1982 noted, 'They were not worried about dying, and when they were issued steel helmets they would not wear them'. He noted they took heavy casualties, but, '...even so, they were very cheery and always making jokes'.[82]

By 1987 the Pasdaran, administered and supported by their own ministry, had become grimmer but also more professional: few would not accept a helmet, but many would wear a green or red bandana and a symbolic wooden or plastic key to heaven around their necks. At battalion level, despite heavy casualties, they were formidable opponents who were skilled in infiltration and the use of light and heavy weapons. However, at divisional and task force level their leaders still had much to learn, especially about all-arms

Most of the T-55s operated by the Iranians as of 1987-1988, were originally captured from Iraq during earlier offensives, especially during the fighting for Khorramshahr, in 1982 – like these three examples (including a Chinese Type 69 with its distinctive side skirts). A number of them suffered additional damage over the following years, to a degree where, by 1988 the Iranian industry was badly lagging with necessary repairs. (Farzin Nadimi Collection)

operations. The core of the Pasdaran remained light infantry with divisions having been re-organised to a dozen rifle battalions and one artillery battalion with a dozen 122mm howitzers or 130mm guns, augmented by 122mm MLRS; a heavy support battalion with 120mm heavy mortars, recoilless artillery, air defence weapons and 107mm MLRS; a small reconnaissance battalion, and a company-size engineer battalion.[83] There were 26 named and numbered infantry divisions each of some 6,500 men together with 43 brigades including special forces, each of about 1,400 men – but, the clerics' ambition was to create a separate modern army to offset the 'conservative' IRIA.[84]

Tactical requirements resulted in the decision that any brigades not expanded into infantry divisions were converted into specialized formations – including six engineer- and two armoured/mechanised divisions in SOHQ, together with one armoured- (each with 40 tanks) and two mechanised brigades (with 20 tanks each).[85] There had also been a substantial expansion in specialized support brigades with four artillery-, two anti-armour-, four air-defence-, and four engineer brigades, while the threat from chemical weapons saw two brigades converted into chemical decontamination units. The Pasdaran naval forces were also substantially increased during the 1980s, and five brigades of marines and SEALs were created together with coast-defence artillery brigades. Pasdaran strength is generally given at around 500,000 although US intelligence estimated only 275,000 were deployed along the western front.[86]

In February 1987 the IRGC was re-organised again: from five directorates created in September 1984 into 15 commands, mostly provincial based, each of which would support specific Pasdaran formations. Curiously, their autonomy had been steadily curtailed as the war progressed and until well into the mid-2000s.[87] Generally, the quality of the Pasdaran formations rapidly declined from 1987 due to the cumulative effects of heavy losses among junior leaders and non-commissioned officers, but also to emigration.[88]

Further to the IRIA and the IRGC, there were also the Gendarmerie of 40,000 – largely consisting of police and border-protection units with counter-insurgency duties in Iranian Kurdistan. They were divided into provincial-based districts; sub-divided into regiments and companies, with most of the men assigned to small posts. In border districts, especially those in Kurdistan, each regiment had a 'strike unit' – or an intervention force – varying from a battalion to a company.

All the branches of the Iranian military have had one severe problem in common: their logistics. A sophisticated, US-developed, computer-supported inventory system was sabotaged during the revolution and it took a great deal of time getting back on track. One of consequences of this success was for the IRIAF to realize it had twice the number of critical spares that it had believed. However, in other services it was the sheer size of the war with Iraq that created immense backlogs at repair centres. In order to speed-up the re-delivery of vehicles to their units, so-called 'cannibalisation' of spares became widespread practice, and especially in regards of sophisticated equipment. Every single hour of 'down time' between major offensive was used to repair damaged or captured equipment, and to re-supply and re-equip units. This, in turn, made it difficult to launch and to sustain multiple simultaneous offensives. Attrition was massive: by 1987, the US intelligence estimated that the IRIA and the IRGC lost 1,000 MBTs, 500 APCs and IFVs, and 550 artillery pieces in the war.[89] Only about 150 MBTs and 120 APCs, 400 guns and 2 million shells and mortar bombs were either refurbished or acquired during the same period.[90] This forced the Iranians to increasingly rely upon inferior equipment of Russian design but Chinese- or North Korean production. The 88th Armoured Division, for example, had to be built-up with Libyan-supplied T-55s and T-62s instead with originally planned Shir Irans. Overall, the war left Iran in possession of some 1,040 MBTs, about 1,400 APCs and IFVs, 630 towed- and 230 self-propelled guns, and about 100 truck-borne MLRS, but

A group of Pasdaran meeting reinforcements arriving on the frontline. (via S. S.)

A typical scene of IRGC troops within recently captured Iraqi positions, during the lull in fighting, in the second half of 1987. Notable is increasing use of steel helmets. (via S. S.)

The diet of Iranian troops on the battlefields of the war with Iraq was rather austere. These two Pasdaran are sharing a can of cherries and some flat bread. (via S. S.)

As in many other wars, reading letters from home – or writing them – was one of favourite occupations of troops on both sides of the Iran-Iraq War. (Photo by Bahman Jalali)

Until the heavy losses they suffered during Operations Karbala-4, -5, and -8 – primarily caused by massive use of Iraqi chemical weapons – the Pasdaran were generally in high spirits and cheerful. This group was photographed during preparations for one of attacks on the Duaiji Line. (via E. S.)

with 70-75% serviceability. A further 400 tubes were stored in unserviceable condition.[92]

By contrast, the Iraqis estimated that Iran still possessed 1,700 MBTs, of which 300-400 were operated by the IRGC, and about 50% were serviceable. Furthermore, the Iraqis noted that the tanks in question had main guns with seven different calibres, which imposed serious supply problems. Both the Americans and Iraqis agreed that the Iranians had 1,400 APCs and IFVs.[93]

Serviceability problems, and maintaining regular maintenance schedules, were also the primary problem of the IRIAA. This entered the war with 864 aircraft and helicopters, but was down to about half this number by 1987 – and many of older types were nearing the end of their useful airframe lives. Actually, the Iranian Army Aviation could still call upon 105 AH-1J Cobras (of which about a third could deploy TOWs), 90 Agusta-Bell 206 reconnaissance helicopters, 210 Agusta-Bell 205 and Bell 214A transport and assault helicopters, and 35 of the Italian-built CH-47C Chinook heavy lifters.[94]

Except for the air force, all other branches of the Iranian military were short on radio communications and navigational equipment. While providing a degree of security, this made C3 extremely difficult.

This perilous military position of Iran was reasonably well-known to the Commander of the US Central Command, Marine Corps General George B. Crist, who accurately informed the Senate Armed Services Committee in March 1988 that Iran lacked the military resources for another major offensive. He said Iran had over-stretched itself in its last assault on Basra and was having problems finding enough new recruits. It had also been seriously weakened economically by the intensified Iraqi air attacks on more than thirty cities.[95]

The Iraqi view of the enemy was revealed to foreign defence attachés in two briefings which showed Baghdad regarded the Pasdaran as the prime threat:

Wreckage of an IRIAA Bell 214A, shot down during the fighting in early 1987. The Iranians carefully recovered all of such remnants: following the war, they were either used for extraction of spare parts, or even completely rebuilt. (Farzin Nadimi Collection)

only half of these were serviceable on average.[91] Curiously, just a few months later, and following information-exchange with Iraqi General Security Intelligence Directorate, the US intelligence agencies corrected their assessments to about 1,800 towed- and self-propelled guns (including about 500 assigned to IRGC's units),

'The Regular Iranian Army was identified as poorly led, badly equipped, secularly motivated and therefore confined to a supporting and diversionary role'.

This must have been a personal disappointment to the British Defence Attaché in Baghdad, Colonel B. Aldridge, who had trained

Starting in 1986, the Iraqi Air Force began exercising constantly increasing pressure upon the Iranian economy. This in turn forced the IRIAF to keep most of its remaining interceptors reserved for the defence of strategic areas such as Khark Island. This F-4E from TFB.6 (Bushehr) was photographed while flying a combat air patrol over a pair of tankers bound for Khark. (Farzin Nadimi Collection)

the Iranian Army for 2½ years from 1976, the last three weeks under the Khomeini regime.[96] One reason why the IRIA was relegated to 'a supporting and diversionary role' was the reluctance of both Pasdaran and Basiji to become involved in static defence: their commanders preferred short offensive operations – no matter how bloody.

Financing the War

To pay for military equipment both sides depended upon oil. Iranian oil exports had been halved in 1986 to some 800,000 barrels a day, but by early 1987 had risen to 1.5 million barrels a day. Refining capacity had also risen to 100,000 barrels a day, but the international price of oil dropped to a record low.[97] As the international price steadily declined both sides ignored the oil cartel's attempts at regulating oil prices through production quotas and actually increased production. In the last quarter of 1986 both sides averaged around 1.6 million barrels per day (MMBD) each month. During 1987 Iranian production for the first three quarters averaged 2.27 MMBD per month, declining to 2.26 MMBD in the last quarter and 2.00 in the first two months of 1988 – by which time the battered and mismanaged oil industry provided only 10% of Gross National Product (GNP; compared with 38% in 1979).[98] By contrast Iraqi production averaged 1.93 MMBD in the first three quarters of 1987, reached 2.56 MMBD in the last quarter and 2.45 MMBD in the first two months of 1988; it provided 40% of GNP by 1987 compared with 50% when the war broke out.[99]

Iraqi exports through oil pipelines steadily rose during 1987-1988 while the so-called 'Tanker War', together with raids on oil targets inland, saw Iranian oil exports by sea adversely affected. With both sides economies in melt-down there were few major arms purchases involving ground forces' equipment in 1987-1988 – apart from one to Iraq from Egypt, agreed at the beginning of 1987, with deliveries from April. This included about 100 T-55s, an unknown number of APCs and towed artillery, four SA-2 air defence batteries, 12 Embraer EMB.312 Tucano trainers and 10 Gazelle helicopters. This was not enough to replace the losses the Iraqis suffered during Operations Valfajr-8 and Karbala-5, which – according to US intelligence estimates – had cost Baghdad 800 armoured fighting vehicles.[100] Iraq's military creditors were growing restive, with the country's debt estimated at $40 billion by the end of the war, while foreign exchange reserves fell from $36 billion in 1980 to $3 billion in 1987 (in comparison, Iran's declined to $5.5 billion).[101] Paris was meanwhile making token delays in delivering equipment, while by March 1988 China was demanding payment for mortar fuses and threatening not to make further supplies if the money was not forthcoming (eventually, Beijing did not carry out the threat).[102]

Nevertheless, Iraq continued receiving substantial quantities of new equipment from earlier orders, and thus managed to increase the total number of its MBTs to 6,600; that of APCs and IFVs to about 4,000; the number of towed artillery pieces to 2,200, and that of self-propelled guns to 300 – in addition to 276 truck-borne MLRS'.[103] Furthermore, in the light of lessons learned on the battlefield the Iraqis began modifying their Soviet equipment; to meet the threat from RPGs they provided their vehicles with appliqué armour (30mm steel plates for T-72 MBTs and multi-layer armour for T-55 MBTs; 35-40mm steel for BMP-1 IFVs), improved passive night sights, and steel 'skirts' to protect the sides of vehicles. Chinese Type 69 MBTs received laser rangefinders. However, adding armour to the T-55 reduced its power/weight ratio from 16 horsepower-per-tonne (hp/t) to 14.7 hp/t.[104] (35).

The Iraqi Forces

According to one estimate, by 1987, out of 2.6 million Iraqi men aged 18-45, almost 1.7 million were in uniform. However, the shallow well of manpower meant many Iraqis had to serve several times, on various fronts, where up to three men per family were deployed.[105] Those in higher education were exempt from conscription until the Faw Campaign when Saddam drafted 125,000 university lecturers and students.[106]

As of 1987, the strength of the Iraqi Army was estimated at 875,000, including up to 480,000 reservists. There were also some 4,800 Border Guards who were used for counter-insurgency duties, which was also a role of the People's Army (al-Jaysh ash-Shabi, also 'Popular Army'). This Baath Party's paramilitary organisation had grown from 75,000 to 100,000 during the war, and while it proved a failure in conventional operations it was perfectly capable of guarding lines of communications and hunting deserters even in the Hawizah Marshes. Between 1985 and 1988 at least 195,000 Iraqis – including a few women (most of whom served as medical staff or in rear echelons) – were recruited, usually co-opted or coerced by commissars, and trained.[107]

The foreign military presence in Iraq remained limited. About 1,200 Soviet, Bulgarian, Czechoslovak, East German, Hungarian and Polish military advisors were present, primarily within local

With Baghdad having a nearly unlimited approach to the international arms market, and dozens of countries being ready to deliver almost everything requested, Iraqis troops were – by far – the better-supplied on the frontlines of the Iran-Iraq War. This soldier was photographed while guarding stocks of small-arms ammo. (Albert Grandolini Collection)

maintenance facilities. France provided some 65 advisors; foremost in relation to various of its arms sales; Yugoslavia had a group of about 100 military advisors (and more than 5,000 civilians) working on further development of hardened air bases; while some 110 Indians, and about 185 Egyptians and Jordanians served as instructor pilots with the IrAF and the IrAAC.[108]

The Iraqi Army was meanwhile organized into more than 40 divisions (Firka), of which five were armoured, two mechanised, and 33 infantry. These controlled a total of 26 armoured, 16 mechanised, 132 infantry, 6 special forces (al-Quwwat al-Khassah), and 16 commando (al-Maqhawer) brigades. The Navy provided another two brigades of marines.[109] Armoured divisions averaged 13,800-14,800 men (against an establishment of 18,500), while the figures for mechanised and infantry divisions were 14,250-15,200 (19,000) and 15,750-16,800 (21,000) respectively. Manpower shortages meant the brigades were also under their authorised strength: in the case of armoured brigades they had 1,800-1,900 against an establishment of 2,400; a problem exacerbated by generous leave entitlements. Some 60 per cent of the Iraqi Army, including the majority of its armoured and mechanised forces, were on the Southern Front.[110]

Baghdad's three original corps (I, II and III) were overstretched as new fronts opened up and four more (IV, V, VI and VII) were created between 1982 and 1986, often by expanding an ad hoc operational headquarters. Also created in Wasit Province on the central front was the reservist I Special Corps – deployed in between II and IV Corps. Each corps had a number of divisional headquarters and reserve brigades augmented by two commando brigades and strong support forces. These included an artillery brigade headquarters, usually with battalions of towed artillery and truck-borne MLRS, an air defence brigade with battalions of 'Gainful' SAMs and light anti-aircraft guns, a reconnaissance battalion with BDRM-2 and APCs, an anti-armour battalion with vehicle-mounted missiles or occasional anti-tank guns, engineer, bridging, signal and chemical defence battalions.[111] There were also four surface-to-surface missile brigades; two equipped with R-17E/SS-1b Scud-C and its al-Hussein derivative (223rd and 224th), one with Luna-M/FROG-7s (225th), and one with Brazilian-made Astros long range MLRS (226th).

An increasingly important feature in Iraqi operations was the IrAAC. Under the command of Major-General al-

In attempt to improve the mobility of their artillery – and exactly like Egyptians about ten years earlier – the Iraqis mounted some of their artillery tubes (in this case a 130mm M1954 gun) atop the chassis of T-55 tanks. (US Department of Defence)

Crew of an IrAAC Mi-25 with their mount (serial 2121) – which belonged to the second batch of this type delivered to Iraq in around 1984. (via Ali Tobchi)

Hakam Hassan Ali, this comprised four wings:
- 1st Wing, based at Kirkuk, supporting I and V Corps;
- 2nd Wing, based at Taji, supporting II and I Special Corps;
- 3rd Wing, based at Basra, supporting III and VII Corps; and
- 4th Wing, based at Amara, supporting IV and VI Corps.

These wings had six attack squadrons equipped with Mi-25s and Gazelles; four reconnaissance squadrons with Alouette III, Messerschmitt Bölkow-Böhm Bo.105s and MD.500MFs; 10 transport squadrons with Mi-8T/MT and Mi-17s; one heavy transport squadron with Mi-6s, and two squadrons equipped with Pilatus PC-7 light strikers (nominally assigned to the Border Guards). Each squadron usually totalled 8-15 aircraft or helicopters, but some units operated up to 35. Each wing controlled three to six squadrons and several detachments. As of 1987, US intelligence estimated the total strength of the IrAAF at 40 PC-7s, 40 Mi-25s and 55 Gazelles, 35 Alouette IIIs, 30 Bo.105s, 26 MD.500s, and 217 Mi-8/17s.[112]

One of most important developments for the Iraqis was the significant improvement of relations with the USA. Washington restored diplomatic relations with Baghdad in November 1984, and grew sympathetic with Iraq: Tehran's virulent hatred of the USA – 'The Great Satan' – prompted the Americans to support 'the enemy of my enemy'. However, for many of the crucial decision-makers in Washington (and their friends in London and Tel Aviv) – and despite the fact that the Iraqis did not accept any kind of 'comrades' (Soviet advisors) at any of their headquarters – the country was regarded as a 'Soviet client' and thus the US support for Iraq remained limited to provision of intelligence and some financing.[113]

The Iraqi chain of command of General Command of the (Iraqi) Armed Forces (GCAF) briefly remained as it was following the changes during Karbala-5 – i.e. under the leadership of Saddam and Defence Minister Adnan Khairallah Talfah (Khairallah). Yet Saddam was not satisfied, possibly feeling his new command team was too defensive. Correspondingly, on 14 July 1987 he instigated another reshuffle. Chief-of-Staff Lieutenant General Saad el-din Aziz shared the fate of his predecessor and was retired after barely six months at this post. He was replaced by commander of the I Corps, Khazraji. Saddam also appointed a new Director of Operations, former Guards Corps commander, Major-General Hussain Rashid al-Tikriti, while his predecessor Thabit Sultan, a former IV Corps commander, was demoted to Brigadier and assigned a brigade.

Khazraji was a very capable officer, and former Military Attaché in Moscow, who recognised passive defence alone would not win the war, and advocated offensives at operational level in order to regain strategic initiative and defeat the enemy. Hussein Rashid appears to have held similar views – which in turn were reflected by his appointment, on 17 November, of former 5th Mechanised Division commander Salah Aboud Mahmoud (Aboud) to command III Corps.[114]

The changes reflected the fact that Saddam had gradually eased his political control and allowed professionalism rather than political reliability to determine promotion. He continued routinely rotating corps commanders to prevent them establishing a power base, but still enabled their work, and the work of their staff, to grow more professional.[115]

Meanwhile, GCAF established fortified forward bases, with airstrips, on all the major fronts and assign to each corps and division command the equivalent of the Red Army's Representative of the General Staff – to assist the commander and monitor the situation for the General Command Headquarters (GCHQ). For example, Qader was attached to Shannan's 11th Infantry Division

Sold as 'training aircraft' to Iran and Iraq alike in mid-1980s, Swiss-made Pilatus PC-7s saw widespread service as combat aircraft in Iraq. Officially assigned to the Border Guards, they were operated by two squadrons of the IrAAC and – as visible on this still from a video – armed with gun-pods and rocket launchers. (Tom Cooper Collection)

already during Karbala-5.

Heavy casualties and the need for technical expertise forced a loosening of Ba'ath Party control, and where once only Ba'athists were admitted to military academies now admission was open to all men provided they had shown no hostility to the Party. Professional and technical schools provided most staff officers although some officers were still selected because of connections to officials or the Party. However, the loosened Party control eased the promotion path for mid-ranking officers.[116].

The improvement in quality was reflected in Colonel Aldridge's annual report of May 1987 when he noted the Iraqis had recently moved 24 brigades in a four-day operation which called for 'road transport and dexterous staff work'.[117] Nevertheless he felt the Iraqi military leadership had made a number of errors:

'For the past four months the greater part of the Iraqi Army and all its strategic ground force reserve have been dragged into a battle of attrition…Other sectors of the front, including the north, had been weakened through losing units rotating into the Basra battlefield'.[118]

He noted that Iran's choice of Basra as the main battle site had proved a major setback for Iraq because it lacked space for tactical mobility and forced the Iraqi Army to conduct static defensive positions with armour used as pillboxes, '…and with no ground-to-air communications for Close Air Support… Close combat has made the extensive use of CW (Chemical Warfare) impossible'.

Furthermore, Aldridge noted that during 1986-1987 the Iraqis had anticipated the main Iranian effort would be east of Baghdad on the central front, and in anticipation of this maintained their strategic reserve in this area. But,

> … it was wishful thinking, the Iranians were not to expose their unprotected 'infantry' to 80 miles of open ground.

In fact, during 1987, Khazraji and Aziz redistributed reserves and by Karbala-5 the strategic reserve, with some 15 brigades of Republican Guards, was in three areas around Basra. Unsurprisingly, these were deployed – with distinction – to recapture Iraqi forward positions during Karbala-8.[119]

Expansion of the Republican Guards

No army can endure a prolonged conventional conflict unscathed. The constant stream of casualties erodes overall quality because the best soldiers – those ready to stand up and fight while risking their lives – are most often the victims too. With no end of fighting in sight the majority are left willing to march in step performing

In 1987, the first Iraqi unit equipped with T-72 Ural MBTs – 10th Armoured Brigade – was transformed into a centrepiece of the Republican Guards Corps. This photograph from earlier during the war shows tankers of the 10th with one of their vehicles. (Albert Grandolini Collection)

A T-72M1 of one of the newly-established armoured brigades of the Republican Guards Corps, as seen in the Basra area, in 1987. (via Ali Tobchi)

Marshal Philippe Pétain with the French Army 70 years earlier – although without any mutinies. Like the poilus, the Iraqi troops were willing to defend their homeland, as the Karbala offensives clearly demonstrated, but at command conferences through-out the war Saddam expressed doubts about their offensive spirit.

Khazraji recognized that self-confidence increases morale – which, like Pétain, he sought to restore through instilling offensive spirit upon his troops. Correspondingly, he began pulling divisions out of the line for re-training. During the second half of 1987 and through early 1988, no less than 96 brigades had been honed sharp. This policy would certainly bear fruit during the summer of 1988 when Iraqi infantry divisions, including one unit of elderly reservists, distinguished themselves in offensive operations.

But autocrats often place greater faith in military organizations which appear to reflect the political-social ethos of the regime. Saddam was no exception. Back in May 1986, he ordered a major expansion of the Republican Guard (al-Haris al-Jamhuri). The result was that this grew to four brigades (1st and 2nd Armoured, 3rd Commando, and 4th infantry) – then commanded by his son-in-law, Brigadier- (later Major-General) Hussein Kamal al-Majid ('Kamel al-Majid'). A year later, Saddam decided to double the number of brigades, and then create eight to ten divisions. Correspondingly, a headquarters for the Republican Guards was established under Major-General Iyad Futayyih ar-Rawi, on 25 July 1987.[120]

Most of the new units and formations were created from scratch, although 10 Armoured Brigade was transferred to the Guards to become 10 Republican Guards Armoured Brigade, while the Army remained the prime source of personnel. However, there was no wholesale transfer of men and units such as the Imperial German Army's creation of *Mobiledivisionen* from existing formations in 1917-1918 – because the Iraqis correctly concluded that this would dilute overall Army capabilities. When the Defence Ministry issued the order to raise a unit it would assign a few officers and administrative

basic duties to survive, but with little enthusiasm and less initiative. Consequently, the successful conduct of war increasingly depends upon the elite minority to act as the spearhead. Unsurprisingly, by 1987, both Iran and Iraq were critically short of such men, and the morale on both sides was generally low.

Iraq's limited manpower meant that after serving their time the conscripts were transferred to the reserves, but then frequently found themselves being drafted back to the front. Thousands went 'absent-without-leave' or even deserted. Incomplete figures suggest up to 5 per cent of Saddam's army came under these categories (see below) by 1987 leaving him in a similar situation faced by

Another new weapon introduced in 1986-1987 was the 122mm 2S1 Gvozdika self-propelled howitzer. They were assigned to armoured divisions of the Iraqi Republican Guard. (via Ali Tobchi)

staff for the headquarters. Once activated the headquarters were assigned further troops, as well as equipment, with unit expansion often accelerated by temporarily assigning companies from Army battalions or brigades to accelerate the process. The Guards attracted both university students and the army's best officers, non-commissioned officers and men, with army officers nominated by Baghdad ordered to report within 72 hours otherwise the brigade or division commander would be punished.[121]

Until the expansion Ba'ath Party membership had been a pre-requisite for joining the Guards. Indeed, the Faw battles of 15-25 February 1986 saw two battalions of the Guards losing 175 killed – all of whom were Party members. With the expansion this criterion no longer applied, but party affiliation was essential for promotion – and political reliability remained a factor in selecting senior commanders. Indeed, political reliability remained a factor in selecting senior commanders such as Brigadier Ahmad Hammash al-Tikriti who was appointed first commander of the 'Hammurabi' Division in September 1986. As with the remainder of the expanded Iraqi Army, the abilities of the new divisions were restricted by the general shortage of fully-trained staff officers.[122]

During 1986, 11 new brigades of the Republican Guards were created and organised into four divisions; Hammurabi, al-Medina al-Munawwarah (or 'Medina') and Tawakkalna all-a-Allah' armoured divisions, and Baghdad as infantry division.[123] The following year another eight brigades were created while 1st Republican Guards Armoured Brigade was re-designated the 17th Republican Guards Armoured Brigade, and two Special Forces formations were created; 'Nebuchadnezzar' Infantry – and the Special Purposes Division headquarters ('SP Division'). The latter was an elite special forces command rather than a traditional division.

In the following months the last three brigades were created to fill out the new divisions and give the Republican Guards the strength of 103,000 men.[124] All these divisions were grouped into the same Republican Guards Corps, initially under future Operations Chief, Major-General Hussein Rashid, and later Lieutenant-General Ayad Futayyih al-Rawi (Rawi) – a Saddam loyalist even after the Allied invasion of 2003.

Units of the Republican Guards received extensive training in standard military disciplines. Troops assigned to them were sent to a vast training area at al-Habbaniyah in al-Anbar Province (separate from the former RAF Habbaniyah), constructed in the aftermath of the Arab-Israeli War of October 1973 using Egyptian, Indian, Pakistani, Soviet and Yugoslav experiences. In addition to the usual training ranges, this area offered enough manoeuvring space for entire brigades, and even divisions, to train simultaneously. The units received not only training for combat in daylight, but by night too, and were lavishly equipped. Kamel al-Majid took great care to ensure that the Guards received whatever they requested.[125] It was this intensive training and strict discipline which moulded men from a variety of backgrounds into formidable combat units aided by superior weaponry and a very well-organised logistic system.

Abu Khalil

'Abu Khalil' – the generic term for the Iraqi soldier – was generally a nationalist that opposed the 'hukm al-malali' ('mullah rule'). However, war-weariness and frequent exposure to combat eroded his nationalism and led to dereliction of duty or even desertions. Furthermore, sharp divisions within the army remained – those between officers and other ranks, between conscripts and volunteers, Army's units and those of the People's Army, commissars and front-line troops, Arabs and Kurds, Sunni and Shi'a, men of urban and rural backgrounds, and between people with different educational standards. The patronage played its part too, and all of this strongly influenced the life at the front.[126] Morale was maintained through divisional recreation areas – which included barbers and cafés – where the men could rest and unwind, but foremost through generous leave entitlements. The latter meant that every Iraqi soldier could enjoy a 7-days-leave for ever 31 days on the frontline. However, this resulted in a situation where up to a quarter of a unit was nearly always absent. Furthermore, officers – who also used their men to perform personal errands – often manipulated the leave entitlement in return for money and favours. Others sold fake documents – like identity papers for absentees or deserters, or documents permitting leave. Such manipulations became so serious that in 1986 the Ba'ath Party Military Bureau – which was attached directly to the Presidential Office – asked Military Intelligence to monitor the practice and discipline of officers and commissars involved.[127] [128]

On the contrary, in the case of the Republican Guards units, there were dramatic changes in this regards. Foremost, officers and other ranks were entitled to significant rewards – including money and consumer goods – for heroism. The rates were for example 1,500 Iraqi dinars (equivalent to US$465 at contemporary exchange rates) for recovering bodies from no-man's-land, while taking a prisoner earned 5,000 dinars (US$1,550). A successful military operation might earn an officer 6,000 dinars or US$1,860, and the most senior officers a Mercedes automobile, while a corporal might earn 1,000 dinars or US$300. Further benefits included land, apartments, cars, and educational privileges – and these were provided to the families of 'martyrs' (those killed in action). However, the families often needed the assistance of the local Ba'ath Party which also intervened when disputes arose between widows and the 'martyr's' parents or siblings. The system was extremely bureaucratic – especially when it came to collecting the salaries of the missing or captured. In practice such financial rewards were rare, with medals and citations more usual, although some medals had social benefits. All awards were approved by Ba'ath Party commissars, who worked along an extremely bureaucratic system: while this created opportunities for both corruption and patronage, commissars were present at every level – from platoon to corps command and training camps – their omnipresence seems to have kept the situation under control, at least during the war with Iran. Some problems were experienced by families of those who fell: they often required assistance of the local Ba'ath Party's branch, which also intervened when disputes arose between widows and the martyr's parents or siblings.[129] Unsurprisingly, an Iraqi writer latter summarized:

Adnan Khairallah (centre) – the highly popular and certainly effective Minister of Defence of Iraq, as seen during a visit to the HQ of the II Corps Iraqi Army, together a Bo.105 helicopter, in 1987. Khairallah was a qualified pilot and often flew PC-7s on his own. (via Ali Tobchi)

Pictured from the left General Sultan Hashim The Minister of Defence, on his left is General Abdul Wahid Shanan Al Rebat Chief of army staff, behind them Major General Abdul Raheem Al Janabi, Commandant of the Military Academy.(Ted Hooton Collection)

> …the experience of conscription, training, and battle brought a generation of men from different social and communal backgrounds together on unprecedented scale and forged a sense of Iraqi patriotism and generational solidarity.[130]

Except for better-paid and – trained – troops, units of the Republican Guards also received a formidable artillery element. By late May 1988, each division had 34 guns – most of these self-propelled pieces – plus two MLRS battalions.[131] Primary equipment of their armoured formations were the recently acquired T-72M1 MBTs, equipped with the 2A46 gun (instead of the older 2A26M), and the 1A40 fire control system (instead of older TPD-K1 laser rangefinder). The T-72M1 had a V-46-6 diesel engine, TPN-3-49 gunner's night sight, and TVNE-4B driver night observation device. It also had improved protection with combination armour on the turret and another 16mm of steel armour plate on the front.[132]

Crises in Morale

Because the well of Iraqi manpower was so shallow, life at the front for Abu Khalil became a lethal kismet of death or mutilation from which the only means of escape seemed to be going absent-without-leave or desertion. The only alternative were self-inflicted wounds which would not arouse official suspicion. Following the Faw Peninsula set-back and a central front defeat at Mehran, the Military Bureau of the Ba'ath Party in October 1986 produced a report on the desertion problem, which concluded the revolution had failed to instil a belief in the Iraqi nation or to break the conscript's traditional loyalty to his clan or tribe or ethnicity.[133] By early 1987 desertion had reached epidemic proportions with some men repeatedly deserting even though they knew their families would suffer. On 28 March 1987, during a discussion on operations in the Basra area, Saddam was informed that 24,952 soldiers had left their positions between 1 December 1986 and 20 March 1987.[134]

Saddam Hussein during a visit to the frontlines of the Iran-Iraq War. (M. H. Collection)

Desertion was most acute on the northern front were there were numerous Kurdish para-militaries serving, while in the central front's II Corps one brigade lost 756 – or a quarter of the men![135] On the southern front the Ba'ath Party Southern Bureau noted that the Faw campaign,

> …resulted in a large number of deserters from the army and they increased the crime in (Basra) by stealing.

In the latter years of the war the Bureau had to deal with 67,522 deserters; of whom 58,943 surrendered in an amnesty, 432 were shot while trying to escape, and 193 were executed.[136]

The regime reacted by holding families as hostages: already since 1982, wives, children and parents of deserters could be jailed, while other members of the family would be denied government employment or access to higher education. In December 1985 a decree stated that wives of those who had been absent for more than six months had to seek a formal separation. This could be annulled if the soldier returned, but a second desertion would see it turned into divorce. To deter desertion, commissar-led, Party-manned, execution squads in combat dress with red armbands, were stationed in the rear. They were always from different regions from the one in which they were stationed. The soldiers deeply resented these men with their clean boots.[137]

Medical attention is a key factor in military morale and the British attaché reported a serious shortage of medical expertise in the battle zone – which frequently led to amputations. His predecessor, Colonel R. C. Eccles, bemoaned the lack of defence sales activity but noted a British company had won a contract for 15,000 pairs of crutches and a follow-on order for 30,000 – although a Swedish company had received a larger order in 1986. In January 1987 General Motors of Canada was asked to quote for 10,000 cars with specifications demanding control by men with one arm (left or right), one leg (left or right), or no legs.[138]

Yet even after six years of war, as Aldridge noted, no wounded were seen in cities and towns. He ascribed this to the Arab tradition of hiding those who were not in perfect physical and mental condition. The seriously wounded, especially the maimed and disfigured, were kept in specialised medical facilities – which locals often described as 'hospital prisons' (although families were allowed to make frequent visits).[139]

Iranian Experiences

Demoralisation was to be found on both sides of the line. Morale was lowest among the IRIA, whose offensive spirit had been steadily eroded by a government which clearly favoured the Pasdaran and regarded the 'Artesh' – as the IRIA is colloquially known until today – with profound suspicion. Ever since 1982, most of army's units were assigned defensive duties on quiet sectors of the front which allowed Tehran to limit their supplies and make little attempt to improve their living conditions.

The Iranians also suffered from poor medical facilities, especially in the front-line field hospitals where many died of wounds and infection. Medical supplies, such as dressings, were allowed to run out entirely before bureaucrats would attempt to replace them. A mortally wounded battalion commander, abandoned without treatment in a provincial hospital, wrote in a final letter to his parents: 'They are killing us'.[140].

While there remained wide-spread support for the goals of the Islamic Revolution a combination of factors slowly eroded morale, especially among the Pasdaran. Curiously – and despite its claim for its rule to be based on popular support – the regime's leadership appears to have been blithely unaware of both the problem and its causes. By contrast Iraqi intelligence began to assemble accurate reports of shaky morale.[141]

Boredom and despair, but also war weariness and heavy casualties, as well as poor protection of Iran's border to Afghanistan and Pakistan in the 1980s, resulted in a widespread and serious problem with drug-addiction (mostly with cannabis/hashish, rather than cocaine/heroin). As early as of 1982, the 21st Division IRIA became colloquially known as, 'The Junkies', between the troops.[142]

Heavy casualties, hollow claims that the martyrs were all in heaven, growing national resentment against incompetence and corruption, inevitably reflected in what was effectively a citizen army – the IRGC – too. What added to the butcher's bill was the selection of many military leaders on basis of religious and ideological purity, rather than professional and organisational ability. The men were quick to identify those with inadequacies, and – reportedly – 'happy to help them find them a fast path to martyrdom'.[143]

The troops were aware of the corruption and incompetence, and all but the most devout Pasdaran despised it. However, although defections from IRGC's unit are known, there appear to have been no execution squads keeping Iranian troops at the front. Furthermore, the nation as a whole did not learn about the problem until after the case-fire of 1988. Then it turned out that while many members of the Iranian Parliament ('Majlis') were aware of individual problems, they remained silent for patriotic, or other, reasons; it was only in September 1988 that they felt free to speak. Combined with reports that he had misappropriated defence funds, this resulted in dismissal of the Minister of the IRGC, Mohsen Rafiqdoust.[144] The worst effect of corruption was the failure to expand military production. However, tales emerged of troops being sent infected sheep meat, ammunition being so poorly stored that it became useless, or the lack of replacement tyres for frontline vehicles while IRGC's depots had immense stocks of the same.

Actually, alarm bells should have run in Tehran already in 1986, or at least by January 1988, when it was announced that a 100,000-strong 'Mohammed Corps' would be formed. Instead of noticing a clear lack of popular enthusiasm despite official propaganda, the system obviously failed to understand, and accept, that the recruitment-drive did not achieve even a third of the aimed-for figure. By that time not just the urban middle classes preferred sending their 16-years-youn sons abroad; even the provincial peasantry was no longer rushing to join the Basiji. Overall, only about 350,000 Iranians volunteered for service with the IRGC in early 1988 – compared with twice that number a year earlier.[145]

Even so, Saddam could not afford to be complacent any more: he knew the Iranians had come back from similar reverses in the past. He was also concerned that the lack of action on the southern front after the spring of 1987 could erode the troops' combat capabilities (see below). This was to prove an incentive for Saddam to seek morale-boosting operations.[146]

Chapter 2 notes

69 Khoury, *Iraq in Wartime*, pp.211 (hereafter Khoury).
70 Mosalla-Nejad pp.61-65
71 General Makki, interview with Ted Hooton, November 2016
72 Buchan p.357; Bulloch & Miller pp.148-149.
73 This paragraph is based upon Eshel's article in Armor.
74 This chapter is based upon DDB-1100-342-86, DDB-1100-343-85 and DDB-2680-103-88, Part II.
75 Bulloch & Morris p.247.
76 Khomeini promotes 10, *Jane's Defence Weekly*, 16 May 1987.
77 Hiro pp.195.
78 Based upon DDB-2680-103-88 Part II pp.10-11. IRIA divisions had four artillery battalions with a nominal 54 tubes.
79 CRRC SH-PDWN-D-000-730. JDW, Mobilisation
80 No Sign of Counter-Attack by Iraqis, Jane's Defence Weekly February 21 1987.
81 Bulloch & Morris pp.244-245.
82 Buchan p.357; Bulloch & Morris pp.148-149; Khoury pp.211 & A. R., interview with Tom Cooper, February 2007
83 See interview with Forouzan.
84 Data on the Pasdaran comes from DDB-1100-342-86 and SH-GMID-D-000-529, material in Iranian publications together with units identified in press releases.
85 Tank strengths from SH-GMID-D-000-529.
86 DDB-2680-103-88 Part II pp.10-11.
87 SH-GMID-D-000-529 & A. R., interview with Tom Cooper, February 2007
88 'Iran tries to remould revolutionary guards', *Jane's Defence Weekly*, 1 October 1988, (hereafter JDW Revolutionary Guards). A 1986 CIA study examined the problems facing Iran's ground forces noting both strengths and weaknesses. CIA-RDP86T01017R000302670001-2.
89 DDB-2680-103-88 p.12.
90 CIA-RDP90T00114R000700800002-2.
91 DDB-2680-103-88.
92 CRRC SH-IDGS-D-000-854
93 See Davis' article on *Iranian Operational Warfighting Ability* p.32; JDW, Mobilisation & CRRC SH-IDGS-D-000-854.
94 DDB-2680-103-88. In February 1979 the IRIAA had 820 helicopters and 44 fixed-wing aircraft (information provided by A. R. and M. T., in interviews with Tom Cooper, April 2009)
95 Bulloch & Morris p.244.
96 Aldridge report, 21 May, 1987 Para 45.
97 Bruce JDW. A barrel is 159 litres.
98 CIA-RDP89S0145000600600001-5
99 Based upon Lessons, Table 9.6. For the economic problems see Hiro pp.109-113, 192, 194 who noted the oil price had stabilised in early 1987 to $15-18 per barrel. See also CIA-RDP89S0145000600600001-5.
100 CIA-RDP90T00114R000700800002-2
101 CIA-RDP89S0145000600600001-5
102 CRRC SH-APGC-D-000-731
103 DDB-2680-103-88
104 Lessons pp.440, 447. See also *Jane's Armour and Artillery, 1996-1997*, pp.48-49 for improved Iraqi armour and Warford's article on tanks.

105 Hiro p.195; Khoury p. 95.
106 Khoury p.32 & DDB-2680-103-88 p.14. The Americans estimated about 20,000 Egyptian and Sudanese volunteers were serving in the Iraqi Army. While exact figures for the Sudanese remain unclear, Egyptian sources indicate presence of special forces, and at least a detachment of the Egyptian Air Force (EAF), including a number of instructor pilots and ground support personnel. Whether the EAF indeed deployed half a squadron of Dassault Mirage 5 fighter-bombers to Iraq, as reported by several unofficial Egyptian, and even some of Iranian and US sources, remains unclear. Finally, large numbers (some estimates go as high as 2 million) of Egyptians are known to have worked in Iraq of the 1980s, some of them in civilian organisations and services supporting the Iraqi Army.
107 Khoury pp.99-100 and information from General Makki. See also Woods, *Mother of All Battles*, p.100.
108 DDB-2680-103-88 p.30
109 In Arabic a brigade is Liwa and brigades are Alwiya. The order of battle is based upon DIA DDB-2680-103-88. CRRC SH-PDWN-D-000-730 87. The US DIA put Iraqi Army strength at 146 infantry brigades, six special forces and 17 commando brigades. The three original Special Forces brigades, 31st, 32nd and 33rd were renumbered 65th, 66th and 68th in the mid 1980s and a flexible number of brigades were created. While they were intended to operate behind enemy lines conducting reconnaissance and precision sabotage operations, in practice by 1987 they were often used as specialist assault troops who also doubled as a reaction force. The distinction is between cat-burglars and smash-and-grab specialists.
110 DDB-2680-103-88, p.14 & JDW, Mobilisation.
111 US intelligence calculated the Iraqis had some 10 battalions of self-propelled artillery with some 180 weapons DDB-2680-103-88 p.9.
112 DDB-2680-103-88 p.16.
113 Nevertheless, Washington permitted the open sale of Bell 214STs and the MD.500 helicopters for 'agricultural use' knowing they would be used for military purposes. Furthermore, Washington did not oppose delivery of South-African made bombs based on US design for Mk.84 to the IrAF – via Saudi Arabia (Sadik, interview with Tom Cooper, March 2005). The Soviet Southern Theatre of Military Operations was estimated in 1986 to have had 26 divisions and 1,800 aircraft capable of invading Iran together with five divisions and 575 aircraft in Afghanistan CIA-RDP86T01017R00050539001-8.
114 General Makki, interview with Ted Hooton, November 2016. Rashid's predecessor, Dhiya ad-Din Jamal, became Director of Ordnance. Khazraji continued serving as Chief-of-Staff Army until August 1990, when he learned of Saddam's invasion of Kuwait on the radio, while driving to the office. Increasingly out-of-step with the regime, he was replaced by Hussein Rashid and then fled to Jordan, in 1996. According to Makki, Defence Minister Major General Abdul Jabbar Shanshall was also kept out of the loop, and Hussein Rashid apparently plotted the invasion of Kuwait behind their backs with Ayad Futayyih al-Rawi – commander of the Republican Guards Corps since 1988.
115 Marashi and Salama p.168
116 Khoury pp 83-85, 97
117 Aldridge report, 21 May,1987 Para 57.
118 Ibid, Para 48.
119 Ibid, Paras 49, 51 & 56. In fact the eastern approaches to Baghdad are open but cultivated terrain with numerous fields, groves, villages and towns. Unsurprisingly, the IRIA developed a contingency plan for an 'all out' advance on Baghdad through exactly this area as early as of 1981. This was presented to the Joint Chiefs of Staff in Tehran at latest in May 1982, but turned down because the IRGC declared it a 'gamble' (T. L., former DIA analyst, interview to Tom Cooper, May 2002). On the other hand, and like many of his attaché colleagues, Aldridge underestimated the value of fixed defences against an enemy lacking armour and artillery. His comment on problems with deploying of CWs was accurate when referring to the FEBA. However, the Iraqis made extensive use of chemical weapons on the Iranian rear, notably during Valfajr-8. In interviews with Tom Cooper, Sadik also pointed out that the Iraqi Army had a forward air controller assigned to every brigade since 1962.
120 Al-Marashi and Salama pp.167-168; Woods (et al) *Project 1946*, pp.111-114, 119 & Jupa and Dingeman's article 'The Republican Guards: Loyal, Aggressive, Able'.
121 *Project 1946*, pp.111-113
122 Khoury pp 85-86, f/n 11
123 American sources suggest these divisions were numbered respectively 1st, 2nd, 3rd and 5th while the 'Nebuchadnezzar' Division was numbered 6th. The majority of former Iraqi officers stress that they were known only by their names – except for the Special Purposes Division, which for some reason was unnamed (the last is sometimes referred to as the Special Forces Division but the Iraqi designation is retained). However – and whether under US influence or not – an increasing number of Iraqi sources are using numerical designations, too.
124 Guards units formed in 1986 were 8th, 9th, 10th Armoured; 14th, 15th Mechanised; 5th, 6th, 7th Infantry, 11th, 12th Cdo and 16th SF Bdes followed – in 1987 – by 18th Armoured; 20th, 22nd, 23rd, 24th, 25th Infantry, 21st Cdo and 26th Naval Cdo Bdes. The naval commando brigade was reportedly trained by Egyptian instructors and was assigned to the SP Division, reportedly designated 'as-Saiqa' (commandos).
125 Hussein Kamel al-Majid would fall out with Saddam and in 1995 fled to Jordan with his brother, Lieutenant-Colonel Saddam Kamel al-Majid. They were persuaded to return in February 1996 but their homes were attacked by Special Forces and both were killed.
126 Ibid, pp. 90-92 and Makki's comments. 'Abu Khalil' was the equivalent to 'GI Joe' or 'Tommy Atkins'. It developed from Khalil (Hebron) where the Iraqi Army distinguished itself during the 1948-1949 War with Israel. Khoury claims the correct name was Abu Tahrir but this was used only for a short period.
127 Khoury pp. 98
128 The French Army soldiers faced similar problems which contributed to the 1917 mutinies. Aldridge (in Para 59) noted that enemy action might mean soldiers staying up to 50 days in the front line. Such cases were rather rare and if, then applicable for the central and northern fronts: in the south, the 31-days rule was rarely exceeded.
129 Comments by General Makki & Khoury pp.84, 88, 96-97, 71, 167-168, 176-177. Some 62,000 Iraqis were taken prisoner by Iranians during this war, of whom 40,000 were repatriated in 1990 and 16,700 by 2003 while 4,600 opted to remain in Iran. The Iraqis released 37,861 prisoners by 1990 (Khoury pp. 103-110). Aldridge, in Para 58, noted that servicemen who had distinguished themselves, families of the killed, and crippled soldiers could at least acquire Brazilian-made Volkswagen Passat cars at cheap rates.
130 Khoury p.83
131 SH-PDWN-D-000-730-87
132 Details from Foss, *Jane's Armour and Artillery 2007-2008*, p.106 &

Juppa and Dingeman article.
133 Khoury, pp91-92 & 99
134 Murray & Woods p. 297.
135 Khoury pp.73, 99 f/n 35
136 Ba'ath Regional Command Council 01-3212-0001-0546/0550 quoted by Khoury pp.75
137 Khoury, pp102-103, 177-178, 2015. Claims that they may have included Sudanese and Egyptian troops appear to be untrue.
138 Aldridge Paras 58, 59; Eccles Para 62
139 Op-cit Para 60. They appear to have been more medical isolation than prison facilities.
140 Bulloch & Morris p.237
141 Murray & Woods p. 297 f/n 36.
142 A. R., former Iranian Army NCO, interview by Tom Cooper, February 2004. Notable is that there appears to have been a minor drugs problem within the Iranian Army already during the rule of the Shah, in 1970s.
143 P. P., veteran of Ramadan Armoured Brigade, IRGC, interview by Tom Cooper, December 2005
144 Rafiqdoust was replaced by Ali Shamkhani who had previously been the Pasdaran ground forces commander (JDW Revolutionary Guards). A year later the ministry was absorbed by the Defence Ministry.
145 Bulloch & Morris pp. 243-244; JDW, Mobilisation. A CIA study of April 1988 noted that the number of volunteers had declined 10% per year since 1985. CIA-RDP89S01450R000200230001-0.
146 See Murray and Woods pp.297-301 for Saddam's concerns about army morale.

3
SADDAM'S FIRST BLOW

Tehran's Karbala debacle raised Saddam's hopes that he could regain prestige with his own offensive and thus end a morale-eroding lull on the Southern Front. Inevitably he looked at the southern Faw Peninsula whose loss he keenly felt. Related thoughts had predominated the front's generals all the time since the summer of 1986.

Although that offensive had always been a political action first and foremost, rather than a military operation, for Tehran the high hopes raised by Valfajr-8 had been rapidly sucked into the peninsula's marshes: neither Kuwait nor Saudi Arabia ceased providing support for Iraq. The Iranians thus attempted increasing pressure: a battery of the 1st Naval Region's 26th Salman Coast Defence Missile Brigade was transferred from Sirri Island to Faw, and reorganized as the 36th Assef Coast Defence Missile Brigade. This unit began firing Chinese-made CHETA YJ-6/C.601 (HY-2 Silkworm) anti-ship missiles at tankers underway off the Kuwaiti coast.[147] Furthermore, a battery of 170mm North-Korean-made Koksan self-propelled guns also crossed the Shatt for this purpose: through its deployment on Faw, it was not only capable of shelling the Iraqi naval base of Umm Qasr, but also reach most of Kuwait.

In the largest urban area, Faw City, the office of the Tehran-backed Supreme Assembly of the Islamic Revolution of Iraq (SAIRI) was established under Hojatoleslam Mohammed Baqr al-Hakim, with members of the exiled Hakim family whose 'military arm' consisted of Hakim's bodyguard under a thug called Abu Ali Mowla. Its offices were used by Pasdaran students who aimed to complete their education at its library. Meanwhile, during the last quarter of 1987, President Khamenei authorised national mobilisation and ordered all the students, mullahs, and civil servants to, 'breathe the smell of the war fronts'. Under cover of the rainy season at the end of the year, wild rumours began making circles about 20 Pasdaran divisions and 200 battalions of Basiji assembling for a new offensive in the south.[148]

From the point of view of the Iraqi military, the elimination of this 'buzzing mosquito' at Faw would have provided significant, strategic level advantages through re-opening the Iraqi approach to the waters of the northern Persian Gulf. At the operational level, it would free troops necessary to reinforce III Corps, and remove a major threat to Kuwait's oil industry – both directly, by eliminating enemy fire bases; and indirectly, by removing the threat of Iranian mines (like the one that damaged the Kuwaiti tanker SS *Bridgeton*, on 24 July 1987, or the US Navy's guided missile frigate USS *Samuel B Roberts*, on 14 April 1988).

Iraqi Preparations to recapture the Faw Peninsula

For Saddam, as one commentator observed: "This was his last chance to rectify these losses that had happened along the borders of Iraq.[149] The work on 'Plan 2' – the recapture of the peninsula – began on 16 June 1986, when a planning cell was established in Baghdad. Presided over by the future Defence Minister Major General Abdul Jabbar Shanshall, this prepared an outline further developed by the staff of Lieutenant General Maher Abd al-Rashid's (Maher) VII Corps. Originally the offensive was scheduled for the autumn of 1986, but this deadline had to be abandoned allowing the plans to be refined in 14 meetings, always chaired by Saddam, and including representatives of the IrAF and the Iraqi Navy, with detailed work by an AFGC planning group with VII Corps.[150]

Saddam was paranoid about secrecy, so the AFGC planning group which he chaired initially consisted only of Guards Corps commander Iyad Futayyih al-Rawi (Rawi), his Chief-of-Staff, and his Intelligence Officer. During the summer of 1987 the cell was expanded to include the Army's Operations Chief Hussein Rashid. However, Army Chief-of-Staff Khazraji was still largely excluded although he did receive an outline briefing. Co-ordination of the planning group's and VII Corps' activities was conducted by Lieutenant General Raad Majid al-Hamdani, who frequently flew between Baghdad and Basra. It was only gradually that additional officers were drawn in, including Lieutenant General Najm-ad-Din Abdallah Muhammad who became Logistics Chief (Deputy Chief-of-Staff for Logistics) in July 1987 and learned of the plan during an AFGC meeting on 27 September 1987.

There was an intensive reconnaissance effort to provide a detailed picture of the berm-based defences as well as the locations of headquarters, batteries and bridges. Iraqi planning was greatly aided by COMINT, while both the United States and the Soviet Union provided intelligence derived from satellite imagery – which showed the defences in considerable detail. Yet most of the reconnaissance work was done by the IrAF, which had been re-organised and re-

A pre-delivery photograph of a Mirage F.1EQ manufactured for Iraq, equipped with the COR-2 reconnaissance pod. (Tom Cooper Collection)

This pair of Iraqi-operated Type-69-II was photographed sometime in late 1986 or early 1987. Notable is the unusual light earth colour used to camouflage the example in the foreground (turret number 31). (via Ali Tobchi)

equipped after Valfajr-8. For this purpose, the air force used aircraft like MiG-25RB, Mirage F.1EQ and Su-22s.

The MiG-25 had an integral AFA-70 or AFA-72 film camera augmented by an AFA A-E/10 and a Romb 4A communications ELINT system and was used more for 'strategic' or general reconnaissance. The Mirages, which assumed the bulk of IrAF reconnaissance tasks from 1986, were equipped with 400 kilogram Dassault COR-2 reconnaissance pods, with four vertically-mounted Omera 35 cameras with focal lengths of 40-600mm, an Omera 70 panoramic camera, or by Sagem Super Cyclope Infra-Red Line Scanner (IRLS) to detect camouflaged targets through their radiant heat. Later these were augmented by Dassault Systems' AA-3-38 Harold and Raphael-TH pods, the former being a 680 kilogram film system with Omera 38 camera (with a focal length of 1,700mm which could provide 2m resolution at ranges of 100 kilometres for long-range optical reconnaissance). The latter, Radar de Photographie Aerienne Electrique a Transmission Hertzienne, was a state-of-the art I/J (also known as X)-Band 10 GHz Side Looking Airborne Radar (SLAR) in a 600 kilogram pod which used synthetic aperture and pulse compression techniques to penetrate up to 100 kilometres, and then transmitted the data in real time data to ground stations. The Su-22 used KKR-1TE/2-54K (Kombinirovanny Konteiner Razvedy) reconnaissance pods. These were 6.79 metres long, 59 cm in width and 58 cm in height, with a loaded weight of 800 kg. They featured an AND a-39 f/100 vertical and oblique 80mm film camera with a focal length of 100mm for use at 500-5,000 metres, and a PA-1 with an oblique camera which had a focal length of 90.5mm, for low level operations up to 1,200 metres.[151] In addition to manned aircraft the Iraqis also used Mirach 1000 UAVs, while the interpretation of film images was aided by the purchase in 1986 of French panoramic stereoscopes.

Front-line units did some probing, notably to determine the location and area of minefields as well as wire entanglements, while Special Forces companies were rotated through VII Corps for reconnaissance behind the enemy lines. Unit 999 – the Military Intelligence Directorate's elite unit specialising in the most sensitive of clandestine reconnaissance missions – usually had its troops operating in the cultivated area.

Most of the troops who had contained the Iranian assault were withdrawn during the summer of 1986, leaving VII Corps with five infantry divisions (2nd, 7th, 14th, 15th, and 26th), and two naval infantry brigades (440th and 441st Naval Infantry Brigades) – for a total of 95,000 troops. Of these, only the 7th and 26th Infantry Divisions, and the two naval brigades – faced the bridgehead.

Plan 22

'Plan 2', aimed to regain the peninsula at minimum cost. Its first draft envisaged the main blow by Maher's reinforced corps with Rawi's Guards Corps in reserve. However, Saddam's desire to test his 'Praetorians' meant Rawi's corps joined the assault force and the Iraqi leader then deliberately encouraged competition between the two corps as to who would take Faw City.[152] Furthermore, an agreement was reached for the two naval brigades to support the Guards, and – later on – to use a heliborne commando brigade in attempt to capture Silkworm launchers deployed at the Cape Bisha (Ras al-Bisha).

The recovery of the peninsula was originally scheduled for October-November 1986, but this was abandoned due to the Iranian Karbala offensives, which forced Saddam to prop up the defence with Guards units scheduled for the assault on Faw. When this threat was contained preparations were resumed as 'Plan 22'.[153]

The planning and operation were de-facto dictated by the terrain. Much of the western side of the peninsula was covered by tidal salt marshes – including a permanently flooded 15-kilometre strip – and the Mamlaha salt beds (64 square kilometre area of extraction ponds sub-divided and surrounded by 1.2-metre high earth bunds). The only permanently firm ground was a six-kilometre wide strip in the east of the peninsula, and even this had numerous irrigation channels through dense date-palm groves and fields in a two to four kilometre belt alongside the Shatt al-Arab. There were three 'hard-topped' (asphalt covered) roads; the highway along the Shatt al-Arab, from Basra to Faw City; another down the middle of the peninsula which later joined the highway; and a third along the Khor Abdullah in the western part of the peninsula from Umm Qasr to Faw City. East of the Basra-Faw City highway was a gravel-topped coastal road running along the edge of the cultivated areas. In between these were countless paths and small, gravel-topped, or

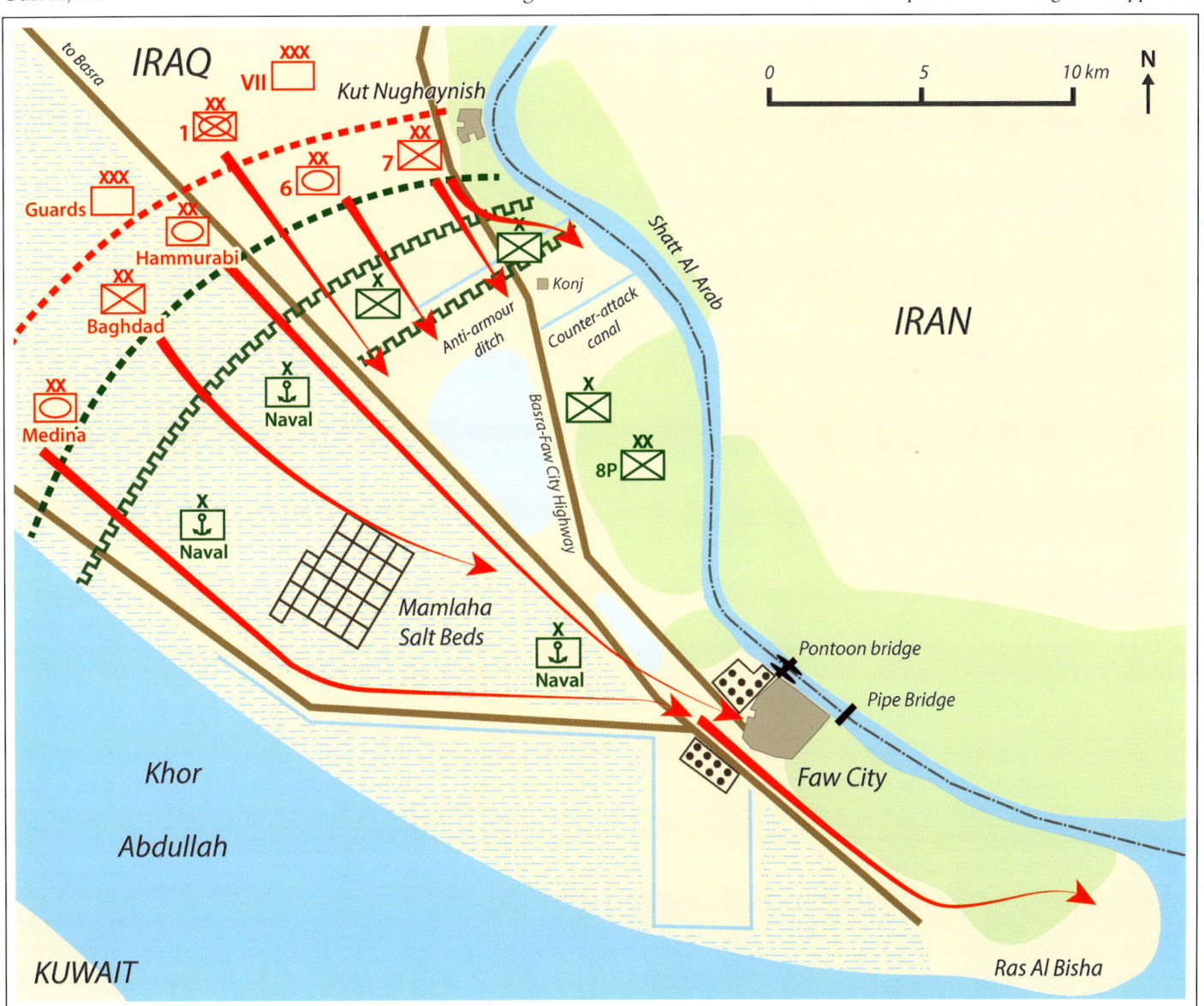

Map 3: The Iraqi liberation of the Faw Peninsula.

beaten earth, roads on embankments. Along the western side of the southern length of the Basra-Faw City highway lay the strategic oil pipeline which provided a degree of cover from fire coming from the salt beds.[154]

The terrain and defences dictated an infantry assault, with mandatory powerful artillery support, in a set-piece offensive like those launched by the Allies in 1917, rather than a Second World War manoeuvre battle. The gunners would first have to neutralise the defences, then support the infantry assault while simultaneously conducting counter-battery work. There was a debate over whether to assault at midnight or in the morning, but all agreed that the assault troops should assemble at night. Eventually the planners opted for an attack after the usual dawn alert when the defenders had been stood down and were having breakfast. It was officially estimated that the offensive would be completed within three days, but there were pessimists – possibly including the 7th Division's commander, Major General Saad Abdul Hadi (Hadi) who feared it would take five days before the whole peninsula down to the Cape Bisha was again in Iraqi hands.

Rawi's main axes would be the central road and the one which ran along the Khor Abdullah from Umm Qasr which he would exploit to swing eastwards like a closing door. The Guards would be the hammer to Maher's VII Corps anvil, the latter advancing southwards between the Basra-Faw City highway and the road running alongside the Shatt.

The offensive was to develop in three phases. After a hurricane bombardment, the two corps would bulldoze their way forward, with infantry first establishing a line beyond the Mamlaha salt beds. They would then insert armoured and mechanised divisions to exploit this success taking the attackers to the outskirts of Faw City – which Maher would then storm. It would be a stand-alone offensive with no immediate follow-on, but its success would determine whether or not there were further offensives on the Southern Front.

Constructing the Battlefield

Hopes were soon dashed of an amphibious assault behind enemy lines, aimed to ease the advance along the Umm Qasr-Faw City road, because Navy commander Major General Ghaib-Hasson Ghaib reluctantly had to concede he lacked dedicated amphibious warfare vessels. From 1977 to 1979 Poland supplied Iraq with four Project 773K ('Polnocny B') class medium landing ships (LSM), giving a nominal 'lift' of a battalion. But at the outbreak of war IrN *Nouh* and *Atika* were being refitted in Basra where they remained for the duration of the war as moored MLRS batteries supporting the Fish Lake Line. The IrN *Janada* and *Ganda* were in Umm Qasr but the former was sunk by AGM-65A Maverick missiles from an IRIAF Phantom in November 1980, while *Ganda* could carry only a company. The shallow waters and wide mud flats made it impossible to use FACs to carry the troops, in contrast to the invasion of Kuwait in 1990.[155]

Starting with 14 May 1986, an equivalent of eight Iraqi engineer battalions – about 6,000 troops – began improving the local infrastructure through expanding and reinforcing roads, adding battery positions and AFV laagers, ostensibly to strengthen the defences. Over time, these units were augmented by personnel and equipment from the Ministries of Housing, and Petroleum as well as Irrigation, and Construction who together provided 350 requisitioned bulldozers and earthmovers. To build roads, each engineer company had up to three earth movers, three bulldozers, six digger vehicles and six road rollers, and could create roads at the rate of up to 3 kilometres per hour.[156] They drained potential

In preparation for their counteroffensive on Faw, the Iraqis constructed an elaborate system of roads, berms, firing ramps, and firing positions for their artillery. The latter (this photo is showing a battery of 130mm M1954 guns) was to play the dominant role during the opening minutes of the attack. (Albert Grandolini Collection)

assembly sites with 16 kilometres of channels and added 1,100 kilometres of roads as well as 16 bridges. To shelter the troops, and provide fire platforms for MBTs, the engineers created 1,060 kilometres of earthworks and would assemble 139,000 cubic metres (111,000 tonnes) of earth, sand and gravel near the major axes to create new causeways through the marshes, while firing positions increased from the second half of 1987.

The planners also examined ways to help the advance and support the capture of objectives using special equipment provided by Iraq Military Industries – which was under Major General Hussein Kamel Hassan. Apart from command tanks, all T-72s could be fitted with a bulldozer blade to push through berms and minefields, while engineers deployed 30-tonne bridges and fabric mats to help soft-skinned vehicles cross the marshes. Each divisional engineer battalion had MTU-20 or, in armoured units, Czech MT-55, Armoured Vehicle Laid Bridges (AVLB) and six GSP ferries, each with a carrying capacity 52 tonnes, augmented by PTS tracked amphibious trucks with a capacity of 10 tonnes.[157]

The Iraqis assembled four Guards divisions (Hammurabi and Medina Armoured, Baghdad and Nebuchadnezzar Infantry) with 19 brigades, and four Army divisions (1st Mechanised, 6th Armoured, 7th and 26th Infantry Divisions) with 24 brigades. The Medina and 26th Infantry Division were assigned largely supporting roles in the forthcoming campaign for which the corps received numerous artillery, engineer, logistic and medical units. The Guards would have to operate in the marshes and had to extemporise solutions to their problem of transiting the marshes or cratered roads. They created raised footpaths from the timber of empty ammunition cases or qugh wood (Khashab al-qugh) ladders. The infantry received snowshoe-like footwear to distribute weight more evenly and each man carried a thick sponge cushion which could be linked up and thrown across a minefield to provide safe passage. Tides moved mines in the marshes and to deal with this movement gabions (baskets filled with stones) were prepared to create a physical barrier on either side of cleared lines.

Because VII Corps would have to advance through the cultivated zone, with its myriad of irrigation channels, it would clearly make slower progress than the Guards whose sector was wider and 'more open' and who had received more intensive training. Maher would also come under fire from across the Dhatt from artillery and mortars which would further restrict his advance. There was extensive preparation with each corps having its own remotely-located training area, resembling their objectives, where troops rehearsed day and night and in all weather conditions. Training emphasised combined arms operations, rapid response to threats, and mutual support among the corps. There were numerous war games for both officers and NCOs using maps and sand tables both to familiarise them with taking their objectives and rehearsing alternative tactics.

Confusing the Enemy

To confuse the enemy, the Director of Military Intelligence Lieutenant General Sabir Abdul Aziz ad-Duri (also 'Sabir ad-Duri'), rolled out a deception plan which began with suggestions of an offensive by IV Corps on the central front in Amarah area. Correspondingly, Major General Sadallah Khalil's Nebuchadnezzar Republican Guards Infantry Division and General Thamir Sultan Ahmad's ('Thamir Sultan') 1st Mechanised Division were both deployed in this area before secretly being sent to the Faw peninsula. Once there, the Nebuchadnezzar was to largely act as the Guards Corps reserve. Other units of the Guards and VII Corps were ostensibly transferred to III and IV Corps, neither of which was informed that these units were not under their command any more. Later they too were quietly sent to the peninsula, with tank transporters and low-loaders sometimes moving several guns at a time.

Baghdad's apparent concern with the northern and central fronts created an Iranian response which played into Iraqi hands. Baghdad's and the international media had long raised the fear of a new Iranian offensive on the southern front and in early 1988 the Iraqis used this as an excuse both for continued preparation work on the Faw Peninsula and for concentrating troops around Basra. Aware of this the Iranians decided to encourage the Iraqis with an ostentatious build-up on the Faw Peninsula as a diversion for a major offensive – Valfajr-10 – around Halabja on the northern front. Trucks, mostly empty, streamed across the Shatt bridges. However, the bluff was quickly detected by Unit 999 and Iraqi COMINT, allowing Baghdad to exploit this both by weakening the Iranian garrison and providing a reasonable excuse for an Iraqi build-up. It also provided a plausible reason to pull Khudayyir's 6th Armoured Division out of its training area and return it to III Corps.[158]

The Iraqis then skilfully turned the concept on its head following the success on the northern front in March 1988 – when Valfajr-10 threatened Iraq's most important hydro-electric project. This threat was regarded seriously by Iraq's military leaders for the first half of the year, but Saddam's gaze remained on the Faw Peninsula. Thus, and in response, Baghdad despatched half the Baghdad Division, reinforced by 24th and 25th Republican Guards Infantry Brigades, to 'meet the threat'. The Iraqi 'concern' was reflected by a well-publicized appearance on the northern front by Defence Minister Khairallah on 16 April 1988, who flew south that evening. But the Guards units barely had time to unpack their kit bags before they were on the way back south, to the bewilderment of the many Iraqi generals unaware of the planned offensive.[159]

Even more bewildered was VI Corps commander, Lieutenant General Yaljin Umar Adil, when he was telephoned on 15 April by Operations Chief Hussein Rashid, and told to take leave even though he knew he was not entitled to any. Part of the Baghdad Division had been under his command and he knew it was undergoing extensive training. Realizing something was 'up', when this division moved south he asked, 'why'? However, fearing a possible arrest for his inquisitiveness, Adil eventually decided to stop asking question and instead began his 'leave' with trepidation. In turn, on the next day he received a telephone 'invitation' to become the Guards Corps alternate commander. He did not arrive until 09:30 on 17 April 1988 but quickly became thoroughly familiar with the plans and would have replaced Rawi if he had been wounded.

Tight Secrecy

The Iraqis realised that with the enemy fully committed in the north there was no better time to strike in the south, and Saddam turned optimistic enough to telescope the first and second phases so the latter would be on Y-Day not Y+1.[160] On 12 April 1988, in conditions of tight security, Saddam chaired a meeting of senior commanders which provisionally scheduled the offensive for 17 April, the first day of the holy month of Ramadan for Islamic Year 1408. For this reason the offensive was re-designated Operation Ramadan Mubarak – the same code name selected by the Iranians for their first offensive on Iraqi soil in 1982. Another advantage of this date was that a number of the defenders were expected to have been withdrawn to go on pilgrimage within Iran, while others might be on leave with their families. The decision was confirmed on 16 April when Saddam met his son-in-law, Guards Director General Kamel al-Majid, Chief-of-Staff Khazraji, the Operations Chief

As of early 1988, the T-55 (and its variants manufactured in Czechoslovakia, Poland and China) still formed the backbone of armoured and mechanised battalions assigned to all of the Iraqi infantry divisions. This example survived most of the war with Iran while retaining its original camouflage pattern in sand and dark blue-green. (via M. H.)

Despite numerous visits to the frontlines and extensive conferences, Saddam kept the timing for a counter-offensive on Faw secret to a degree where even the most important of involved generals did not know when would this start. (via M. H.)

Hussein Rashid, and Intelligence Chief Aziz ad-Duri. Saddam arrived with the date to launch the assault, worked out previously by the army staff, and fearing the room might be bugged wrote it down on a piece of paper which he passed around the room. This set Y (Yom) Day for 17 April with S (Sifr or Zero) Hour at 06:30 and after the others agreed, Saddam tore up the paper and sent word south.

He and Khairallah then flew to the General Command South Operations Centre which opened on the outskirts of Basra at 23:00 on 16 April and included the Directors of Artillery and Engineering, representatives of all arms and associated commands and featured extensive radio and land line communications. Each corps received one of Saddam's sons, nominally to show the nation's leaders were at the front, but also to act as personal observers as division and brigade commanders were informed of S-Hour/Y-Day only 20 hours beforehand and battalion commanders even later. But before dawn the assault force, with a nominal 183,000 men, 910 MBT, 1,100 guns and 100 attack helicopters was ready. Extremely tight security reasons led to the maintenance of the generous leave entitlements and thus many of involved units were at least 10% understrength.

Assembling the Strike-Force

The assembly of the assault forces, organized by Logistics Chief Abdallah Muhammad under tight security, had begun on 13 April 1988. Half of the assault force brigades began assembling, together with 40 artillery (two self-propelled) battalions and thousands of tonnes of supplies. Their movement was concealed by four days of poor weather.

The assault corps were organised in echelon with Rawi's Guards Corps first having Baghdad Infantry and Medina Armoured Divisions, together with 26th Infantry Division – the last largely for consolidation – while the Hammurabi Armoured Division was in the second echelon. The Nebuchadnezzar Infantry Division was in the potential third echelon, but although available as a tactical reserve, many of its brigades – together with part of Brigadier Waad Allah Mustafa Hanoush's (Mustafa Hanoush) Republican Guards SF Division – were assigned to the other guards divisions.[161] This reflected the Guards' shared organisational flexibility: they actually inherited this practice from the experience with the Army turning its divisions into task forces whose strength could be modified to meet unexpected situations or perform new tasks.

The Baghdad Division, under former 11th Infantry Division commander Lieutenant-General Abd-al-Wahid Shannan ar-Ribat ('Shannan'), and Medina under Lieutenant-General Ahmad Ibrahim

A reconnaissance photograph taken by an Iraqi MiG-25RB and showing one of the Iranian pontoon bridges spanning the Shatt al-Arab. (Ahmad Sadik Collection)

Hammash ('Hammash'), had 11 brigades while the follow-up forces of Lieutenant General Ibrahim Abd-Al-Sattar Muhammad's ('Sattar') Hammurabi would follow up with four brigades (see Table 4 for order of battle during the Operation Ramadan Mubarak). Major General Sadallah Khalil's Nebuchadnezzar remained in reserve. Rawi thus had 67,500 men with 315 MBTs, while Maher's VII Corps had 101,500 men with 285 MBTs.

The latter was also organized into two echelons. The first was Khudayyir's 6th Armoured Division and Hadi's 7th Infantry Division with a total of 15 brigades. The second echelon consisted of Major General Thamir Sultan's 1st Mechanised Division (transferred from IV Corps) with six brigades. They were supported by 31 artillery (two self-propelled) battalions and, six MLRS battalions with BM-21s and Astros, augmented by five batteries of Chinese 107mm light MLRS. There were also 12 batteries of 120mm heavy mortars, and a battalion of Frog-7 surface-to-surface missiles. This gave some 1,160 x 105mm, 122mm, 130mm and 152mm tubes, 140 MLRS and 72 heavy mortars.[162]

A Lonesome Outpost

Following the heady days of Valfajr-8, the Iranian garrison on the Faw had been steadily stripped, until it was down to less than 20,000 troops and 100 MBTs. The IRIA troops were the first to re-cross the Shatt during the spring of 1986, followed by both Pasdaran task force headquarters and all seven divisions for eventual commitment to the Karbala offensives in summer of the same year. Iraqi intelligence calculated that there were two Pasdaran divisions and a naval brigade on the peninsula, deployed in echelon with four brigades on the front line and three deployed south of the Mamlaha salt beds. Actually present was only the 8th Najaf Ashraf Division IRGC – whose three brigades returned to Faw after Karbala-8, three naval brigades of the Pasdaran, and about 1,000 Basiji. Two of Najaf Ashraf's brigades were in the front, with the third and two naval brigades acting as reserve in the rear. These troops were supported by some 20 batteries with 114 guns, including a battery of Koksan self-propelled 170mm tubes and 13 MLRS, all augmented by the 94th Sha'ban Air Defence Brigade IRGC, a battalion of 98th Sahib az-Zaman Engineer Division, and members of the 26th Salman Coast Defence Missile Brigade.[163]

Iraqi deception plans appear to have had some success because from late March 1988 many of the Iranian artillery-batteries were withdrawn from the Faw Peninsula, together with some Pasdaran units. The remaining men were mostly low-grade older troops and volunteers who had little or no preparation for gas attack. They occupied an extensive defensive system built after the capture of the peninsula and based upon flooding and berms, but lack of manpower meant that numerous positions were incomplete.[164] Berms running north-to-south were designed to channel enemy armour while those running east-to-west were resistance-lines, often studded with bunkers and dugouts. Dozens of earth ramps were built so MBTs could augment the defender's firepower. To further channel an Iraqi assault using the Basra-Faw City highway as an axis, parts of the western peninsula were flooded.

There was a buffer zone some three kilometres deep between the Iraqi positions and the first line of defence, and in the east the attacker would have to cross a kilometre of inundations 0.6 metres deep. These areas, and the marshes in front of the first line of defence, featured extensive barbed wire entanglements and minefields. A double line of west-east berms up to 50 metres apart and studded with bunkers and dug-outs ran right across the peninsula and was the first line of resistance. On the eastern end, some 350 metres behind these defences, lay a six-kilometre-long flooded anti-armour ditch, between 25 and 60 metres wide, covered by bunkers and dug-outs, artillery and AFV positions, and which acted as a second line of defence.

Equipped with a hodgepodge of vehicles and equipment of US (M113 APCs), Soviet (BMP-1 IFV), East German (W50 truck), Chinese, and North Korean origin, the Pasdaran of Najaf Ashraf Division were not only outnumbered, but also hopelessly outgunned by attacking Iraqi forces. (Tom Cooper Collection)

One of the IRGC's artillery batteries deployed at Faw was equipped with North Korean-made Koksan self-propelled guns. (via S. S.)

Table 4: Order of Battle for Operation Ramadan Mubarak, April 1988		
Corps	Division	Brigades
Iraq		
Republican Guards Corps	Corps Troops incl. Republican Guards Corps Artillery Brigade	
	Hammurabi Armoured Division Republican Guards	17th Armoured, 15th Mechanised, 12th Commando, 20th Infantry Brigades Republican Guards
	Medina Manarwah Armoured Division Republican Guards	6th Infantry, 10th Armoured, 11th Commando, 16th Special Forces Brigades Republican Guards; 440th & 441st Naval Infantry Brigades
	Baghdad Infantry Division Republican Guards	4th, 5th, 7th Infantry Brigades, 3rd Special Forces, 21st Commando Brigades Republican Guards
	Nebuchadnezzar Infantry Division Republican Guards	8th & 9th Armoured, 19th Commando, 22nd & 23rd Infantry Brigades Republican Guards; 110th & 11th Infantry Brigades
VII Corps	Corps Troops, 1st & 2nd Commando Brigades of VII Corps; VII Corps Artillery Brigade	
	1st Mechanised Division	1st & 27th Mechanised, 34th Armoured, 102nd, 108th, 701st Infantry Brigades
	6th Armoured Division	16th & 30th Armoured, 25th Mechanised, 14th, 95th, 104th, 107th, 429th, 802nd Infantry Brigades
	7th Infantry Division	19th, 27th, 38th, 39th Infantry, 66th & 68th Special Forces Brigades
	3rd Wing IrAAC	
	4th Wing IrAAC	
Iran		
	8th Najaf Ashraf Division IRGC	3 brigades
	104th Emir al-Mu'minin Naval Brigade IRGC	
	105th al-Kawthar Naval Brigade IRGC	
	106th Sajjad Naval Brigade IRGC	
	94th Sha'ban Air Defence Brigade IRGC	
	2nd Combat Support Group IRIAA	

About a kilometre behind that was a similar ditch, 'The Counter Attack Canal', some 40 metres wide which was designed to be the jump-off point for counter-attacks directed with the aid of a chain of 20-metre-high observation towers. Within the marshes the Mamlaha salt beds had been turned into another second line of resistance. Behind these positions the eastern approaches to Faw City had been restricted through two flooded areas around the Basra-Faw City highway. One was 3.4 kilometres long and 1.8 kilometres wide; the other – just north of the city – was 2.5 kilometres long and up to 1.5 kilometres wide. A smaller inundation and a 40-metre-wide flooded ditch covered the approaches from the west. The defences were controlled from a headquarters in Faw City linked by underwater landline and a microwave relay tower to Iran. Physical communication with the Iranian homeland was across the Shatt, which the winter rains had raised to its highest level since 1954.[165]

The garrison was supplied by a fleet of some 1,500 small boats and the two bridges; a pontoon bridge north of Faw City, and a bridge south of the city, while at the time of the Iraqi attack work was under way to build another bridge into Faw City. This was similar to the 900-metre-long so-called 'pipe bridge' at Be'ssat, south of Faw City, which was constructed from two layers of oil pipelines and Styrofoam, laid so the tides flowed through them, and whose roadway could accommodate MBTs. A Pasdaran division and 3rd Brigade/92nd Armoured Division IRIA were in reserve ready to cross the Shatt and the IRIAA had some 40-50 helicopters ready to support operations in the south.

The Iranians probably heard the increased noise raised by convoys of newly arrived vehicles, but rain or drizzle from 10-14 April prevented detailed observation. There are claims that from 14 April there was a comprehensive Iraqi programme to jam enemy radars but the accuracy of this claim is uncertain. It is only certain that the Iranians were taken by surprise: their intelligence may have received some indications of Iraqi plans, but any warnings they passed on appear to have been ignored. The first intimation of the offensive came at 05:30 as Iraqi Special Forces began to attack the pontoon bridges across the Shatt which, from 05:45 were also engaged by Iraqi guns, with a battalion assigned to each bridge. Finally, the southern bridge was cut in two by a pair of IrAF's Su-

22M-4s, which deployed Kh-29 (AS-14 Kedge) laser guided missiles for this purpose.[166]

Operation Ramadan Mubarak

A 45-minute bombardment by guns, MLRS and mortars opened a relatively cool day with a maximum temperature of 34° Centigrade with a 29 kilometre/hour wind. The first berms disappeared under a curtain of fire and steel from most tubes while 130mm and 155mm guns, sometimes aided by observation helicopters, engaged batteries, troop concentrations and headquarters. Iraqi artillery benefited from improved training, moving more quickly in response to requests from the front, and efficiently shifting and concentrating fire on centres of resistance. The Iraqis also augmented their Brazilian Astros II SS-30 MLRS with 18 SS-40, each vehicle firing 16 x 152 kilogramme 180mm calibre rockets up to 35 kilometres, with a cluster munition warhead of 20 anti-armour/anti-personnel bomblets.[167]

In addition to conventional shells the Iraqis made extensive use of chemical warheads: mortars, guns and BM-21 MLRS were estimated to have fired up to 2000 warheads, while the CIA estimated that about 100 tonnes of chemical agents were used in the bombardment contaminating the Shatt. The Iraqis especially targeted the rear areas because the support troops had little chemical warfare defence training and little in the way of protective equipment.[168]

The US Defence Intelligence Agencies' Lieutenant-Colonel Rick Francona, who had confirmed the use of sulphur mustard gas ('Agent HD') and Tabun, or Agent GA, semi-persistent nerve agents from 1983-1984, now reported the use of Sarin, or Agent GB, non-persistent nerve agents. During his visit to the peninsula after the battle he discovered numerous atropine injectors and decontamination fluid on vehicles, as well as the absence of insects and birds. His report to Washington led to a brief suspension of co-operation with the Iraqis. Towards the end of the war the former head of Iraqi military intelligence, General Wafiq as-Sammarai, claimed the campaign was the first use of Agent VX – a persistent nerve agent which surprised and terrified the defenders, and which necessitated the equipment of the Iraqi troops involved with both atropine injectors and special tablets to counter the effects.[169]

However, several reports suggest a changing wind blew some nerve gas into the Iraqi lines, possibly those of 7th Infantry Division, reportedly killing almost 200 and forcing the survivors to wear gas masks which, in warm weather, proved extremely fatiguing.[170]

The IrAF and IrAAC also delivered chemical agents, the former using 250 and 500 kilogram bombs with chemical agents, reportedly including VX, but also mustard gas which could be spread 100 metres from the point of impact. Mi-8 helicopters, operating in teams of three, carried either bombs with 220 litres of chemical agent (usually nerve gas), or spray tanks with a capacity of 1,000 litres. Nevertheless, most of the IrAF ordnance consisted of 'iron bombs': about 45 fighter-bombers and helicopter gunships used these to target headquarters, key batteries and the Iranian approaches to the pontoon bridges. The IrAF committed five squadrons in direct support of the offensive; during the day 'Saddam's Falcons' would fly 330 sorties and drop 655 tonnes of bombs, as well as 13 guided air-to-surface missiles, in missions which included interdicting enemy road and rail communications in south-western Iran. The IrAAC would fly 218 gunship sorties on the first day.[171]

The roar of the bombardment concealed the Iraqi troops' initial movements and this was further obscured by extensive smokescreens as well as clouds of gas. Mine clearance was an important role and brigade engineer companies had Soviet- and Iraqi-made hand-held, and Soviet DIM vehicle-mounted, detectors although few were effective against non-metallic mines.[172] They could use the traditional method of lifting mines with hand tools or the Soviet UR-77 rocket-propelled line charge trailer which could clear a 90-metre long lane, 6-8 metres wide, from a distance of 150 metres. Bangalore Torpedoes were used too. Each rifle company had an 8-12 metre wide path marked with distinctive coloured flags. Armoured and mechanised units had Russian-built tank-mounted KMT-4 mine ploughs (one per platoon), and KMT-5 mine rollers (one per company).[173]

The infantry were close behind them ready to suppress enemy fire with their heavy weapons which augmented the artillery with great success. When the guns switched to a rolling bombardment on the enemy's second line, at 06.30hrs, the Iraqi infantry were quickly into the first berms, many were breached with the remainder pock-marked by shell holes and covered with stunned survivors and the dead. Rawi's guardsmen faced more formidable problems advancing through the marshes to overcome the first defensive system and then the heavily defended Mamlaha salt beds. Hammash's Medina Division advanced in two echelons on the Iraqi right wing along the coastal road and shoreline from Umm Qasr to Faw City, with Shannan's Baghdad Division its left. Yet within six hours Rawi had almost all of the first berm line, apart from the coastal section where 16th Republican Guards Commando Brigade – from the Republican Guards SP Division – made slow progress through waist-deep water while advancing bare-footed and partially dressed.

Hammash's centre and left – 6th Republican Guards Infantry and 11th Republican Guards Commando Brigades, supported by 10 T-72s – made faster progress and 6th Republican Guards Brigade swung south to isolate the enemy coastal defences. In their rear, engineers quickly repaired the road to help insert 10th Republican Guards Armoured Brigade, which made such rapid progress towards Cape Bisha that plans for the two navy brigades to make an amphibious assault on the peninsula's southern coast were abandoned and instead they accompanied the tanks.[174]

There was fierce resistance from the Iranians, who used RPGs extensively, forcing some tank crews to use personal weapons to drive them off, but the tanks eventually overran the southernmost Silkworm battery with the assistance of a naval brigade. The rest of the division followed through and within 14 hours had secured the southern coast; with the Iraqi flag being raised over Cape Bisha at 19:00 on 18 April 1988. To their disappointment, the Iraqis found the coast defence and surface-to-air missile sites all empty.

Meanwhile, 6th and 11th Republican Guards Brigades masked the Mamlaha salt beds to support Shannan's Baghdad Division, which brought up its reserves and stormed the salt beds in an intense close-quarter battle, with anti-armour missiles used as 'bunker busters'.

Plan 22 had envisaged the Medina and Baghdad Divisions completing the conquest of the outer defences by the end of Y-Day, opening the way for Sattar's Hammurabi on Y+1. But at noon on Y-Day Saddam rang Sattar and informed him his mission was now to take Faw City. Sattar saw his opportunity, drove back to the Centre and pressed to bring his division forward ahead of schedule. The two Guards division-commanders fully supported him and persuaded Saddam to agree, and during the early evening Hammurabi was brought into the line north of the salt beds. It was substantially reinforced with all of the Nebuchadnezzar Division's infantry and commandos, who arrived after a forced march of 27 kilometres through the marshes carrying all their equipment.

Sattar attacked at 20:00 on Y-Day, fighting his way down the Basra-Faw City highway led by 20th Republican Guards Infantry Brigade, while 12th Republican Guards Commando and 19th Republican Guards Infantry Brigades – together with 17th Republican Guards Armoured Brigade – isolated the town from the south by 14:00 on 18 April. While Sattar planned a full-scale assault led by 12th and 20th Brigades, Khairallah – realising the scale of the enemy collapse – urged him to send just 20th Brigade into the city, but immediately. The unit jumped off at 15.00hrs and – later aided by the other brigades – took it within an hour. The 4th Republican Guards Infantry Brigade then became the garrison.

Khudayyir's Problems ...

The first day's success encouraged Baghdad to accelerate the operation and on the night of 17 to 18 April 1988 Maher was shocked to receive a call from Saddam informing him that the honour of taking Faw City would now go to Rawi's guardsmen. In a back-door attempt to flaunt Saddam's order, the VII Corps Chief-of-Staff Major General Qaidar Mohammad Saleh, rang his opposite number, Major General Ibraheem Ismael, and sought permission to take Faw City. But Ismael refused, arguing it was Saddam's order. Salt was rubbed into the wound when the Guards banned a preliminary bombardment by VII Corps artillery.

The decision taken by Saddam and Khairallah was made after telephone consultations with Maher, and was neither an attempt to increase the regime's prestige nor a personal snub: it reflected VII Corps' weak performance compared with Rawi's guardsmen – despite opening with great promise.

Although Maher advanced across firm ground he had first to traverse a mine-strewn no-man's land with steel obstacles, old palm trunks and battle debris ranging from wrecked AFVs to anti-armour missile guidance wires which could tangle wheels tracks. Maher's left also had to fight through the palm groves of the cultivated area and their numerous irrigation ditches, which could provide enfilade fire into his spearheads. A further complication was that he was confined to two axes; the Basra-Faw City highway and the coastal road running through the palm groves, so that delays caused congestion. Maher's artillery preparation, directed by Brigadier Abd al-Hadi Mohammed Saleh, may have been judged inadequate, for the gunner would be dismissed on 18 May 'for not fulfilling his set duties according to the Blessed Ramadan plan...' and also 'for not taking to task the commanders who did not fulfil their duties correctly...'

Nevertheless, Hadi's 7th Infantry Division and Khudayyir's 6th Armoured Division rapidly captured the first berm line – in spite of slow progress through the palm groves under increasing mortar, artillery and MLRS fire from across the Shatt, which caused severe congestion along the coastal road. One of the infantry brigade commanders became increasingly pessimistic and claimed his unit was 'finished', but Khazraji came over to Maher's headquarters to find out what was slowing the advance and soon dismissed the demoralised brigade commander. Khazraji believed he had solved the problem, but 7th Division's progress remained glacial and by the end of the day it had still not reached its Y-Day objectives.[175]

The lack of progress effected the advance of Khudayyir, who would later claim he was ultra confident of success and had six infantry brigades in addition to his integral armour. His confidence was well-placed. He took the first berm in 12 minutes, aided by a tank company he had moved right up to the berms. Ironically Maher did not at first believe Khudayyir's report, but the latter just continued pushing: he sent 107th and 429th Brigades up to the 'Counter-attack Canal' where they were exposed from the east. Further in the rear, 16th Armoured Brigade was held up at the anti-armour ditch because bulldozers had difficulty pilling up the soft sand to create a causeway.

Eventually Khudayyir's tanks crossed, but he had now fallen behind schedule. In an attempt to make up lost time, and gambling on enemy demoralization, he brought up his wheeled BTR-60

Although involving quantitatively and qualitatively far superior forces, and although proceeding at a high pace, the Iraqi counter-offensive on al-Faw was anything but a one-sided affair, especially on the eastern side of the peninsula, as mines and Iranian anti-tank teams still managed to knock out a number of Iraqi Army's tanks. (Farzin Nadimi Collection)

APCs which had better traction in the sand. Heavy fire from the palm groves on his left – where Iranians were still fiercely resisting Hadi's 7th Infantry Division – created a space up to 300-metres wide and the 107th Brigade had to enter the palm groves to shield his left. Khudayyir's advance eventually picked up pace and was joined by 30th Armoured Brigade, but at 00:35 on 18 April Saddam, fearing that Maher would take Faw City, ordered him to stop on exposed ground forcing the brigades to go into laager for the night. At dawn the 30th Armoured Brigade renewed its advance while 25th Mechanised Brigade was brought up to relieve 16th Armoured Brigade. At noon, they were all ordered to withdraw because of Saddam's order and this ended Khudayyir's contribution to Ramadan Mubarak.

… and Maher's final Push

Meanwhile, Maher tried to break the impasse on his left by bringing up his second-echelon formation, Thamir Sultan's 1st Mechanised Division (whose tanks had been providing fire support for the other divisions). It had been scheduled in the second and third phase operations but now crossed the main ditch to advance on a three-brigade front and assigned one of its infantry brigades to support 7th Division. However, Khudayyir's advance exposed his right as it tried to cross the 'Counter-attack Canal' while craters and un-cleared minefields restricted AFV movement. Thamir Sultan decided to use the remnants of the oil pipeline west of the highway to cover his advance but first brought up tree trunks and 20,000 filled sandbags to repair his communications, while engineers built ramps as fire platforms for MBTs and lifted mines around the highway. The 7th Division had three brigades in defensive positions (including 27th and 102nd Infantry), which 1st Mechanised Division took over, together with its three integral brigades, and he learned that 6th Armoured Division had sent an infantry and a commando brigade into the palm groves.

There was fierce resistance from the former Iraqi strong point which the Iranians called the 'Konj' (see Volume 2), and this stopped a VII Corps' commando brigade which suffered heavy losses. At 09:00 on 18 April, 7th Division finally secured the last of its Y-Day objectives and Maher now ordered Thamir Sultan to assume operational command of its brigades and resume the advance; for which he received the battered VII Corps' commando brigade. Sultan moved 102nd Infantry and 34th Armoured Brigades to cover 6th Armoured Division as congestion built up on the highway behind, due to Iranian mortar fire, and then decided to use 1st Mechanised Brigade as his spearhead, to outflank the Konj and reach the next anti-armour ditch. Moving out at dawn, his units reached the pontoon bridge al-Maamir, which had been destroyed by the IrAF and which was held by Guard Special Forces. Meanwhile, the 27th Mechanised Brigade was brought up and drove down the coastal road only to be stopped 1.5 kilometres from Faw City when Khazraji rang to remind him of Saddam's decision and ordered Sultan to mop up the palm groves – although this duty was soon passed to the newly arrived 2nd Infantry Division which had been hastily brought in to secure the eastern flank.

It was another comment on Maher's poor performance that Rawi was assigned the task of securing the two bridge sites. Part of 3rd Republican Guards SF Brigade was flown into the northern site, but encountered no resistance as they captured a few exhausted and naked Iranians on the shore where they had tried to swim the Shatt. Rawi had also planned to take the southern Pipe Bridge at Bessat, and on the evening of 17 April planned an air assault by his

A Soviet-made Kh-29 (AS-14 Kedge) guided missile, as used by Iraqis to knock out Iranian bridges spanning the Shatt. (US DoD)

reserve 21st Republican Guards Commando Brigade, but the plan was abandoned by midnight due to bad weather.

The End

From the Iranian point of view, the Iraqi assault caused a catastrophe; the opening bombardment decimated the first defending echelon on the berms and inflicted heavy losses on the second echelon, while chemical weapons disrupted the rear echelons. The use of new gases especially stunned the defenders and prevented them from regrouping.[176] Massively outnumbered and outgunned, the defenders lacked heavy weapons; TOW-teams did knock out a number of MBTs, but spent their ammunition stocks very soon too. The palm groves provided some cover, but with Iraqi pressure growing the commander of Najaf Ashraf was left without a choice but to order a fighting withdrawal towards the bridges. While some troops continued to fight desperately news of the northern bridge's destruction further demoralised the defenders and the retreat became a rout. Jostling crowds of men fled across the damaged Pipe Bridge and in the panic some fell, or were pushed off, and drowned. Only then did the Pasdaran issue a demand for top cover from the IRIAF, but – taken by surprise – the latter was unable to provide more than 42 CAS sorties. F-4 Phantom IIs from Bushehr flew 20 top cover sorties for the final retreat on 18 April. Reports from involved Iranian pilots indicate they felt 'drowned in the sea of Iraqi aircraft': the IrAF was present above the battlefield in such numbers, that there was no chance of success in air combats.

'Ramadan Mubarak' achieved its objectives within 35 hours. Nevertheless, the Republican Guards still suffered 1,086 casualties. Total Iraqi casualties were probably about 4,000 men and 20 AFVs while the Iranians probably suffered 5,000 casualties and 2,000 men taken prisoner, with the loss of all their heavy weapons. A delighted Saddam gave his top commanders Mercedes automobiles and on 19 April he went on a pilgrimage to Mecca. That day Rawi's corps was withdrawn northwards and Maher was given total responsibility for the peninsula. He remained bitterly and volubly disappointed at being thwarted at Faw City and, despite being father-in-law to Saddam's youngest son he received only minor awards. When he continued protesting he was replaced by Lieutenant-General Mohammad Abdul Qader and placed in the reserve Office of the Warriors (Deirat al Muharebeen) where he retained all his privileges.[177]

Iraq's Navy commander, General Ghaib, was also disappointed as his only hope of winning glory was dashed. Nevertheless, he was less vocal. He had committed most of his surviving 41 FACs, patrol boats, landing craft and hovercraft as well as a small squadron of

Super Frelon helicopters from Umm Qasr.[178] FACs claimed to have hit one of three Iranian vessels approaching the peninsula and the Medina Division received fire support from one of these vessels and the coast defence batteries. IrAF Super Frelon helicopters under naval operational control were primarily deployed for maritime surveillance, although two were kept in readiness armed with AM.39 Exocets for anti-shipping operations.[179]

The defeat, coming after years of supposed victories, was a severe blow to Iranian morale. It took place at a politically sensitive time: Khomeini was seriously ill, while Tehran had complacently assumed that years of defensive strategy had left Baghdad incapable of a major offensive. The deep divisions between the regular forces and the Pasdaran re-opened, with each side blaming the other for the disaster and the search began for scapegoats. A number of IRIA and Pasdaran commanders were dismissed, with the clerics' biggest scalp being that of the Chief-of-Staff of the Armed Forces Brigadier General Ismail Sohrabi. He was replaced by his 42-years-old deputy, Brigadier-General Ali Shahbazi and relegated to the position of 'military consultant' to the Supreme Defence Council.[180]

Interestingly, while other clerics were blaming top regular military commanders for the defeat, Khomeini criticised all the leaders of the armed forces for 'becoming too arrogant', driving even Rezai into public admission of making mistakes. Nevertheless, the Pasdaran commander in the south, Ali Saleh Shamkhani remained in place and in September 1988 became the Minister of the IRGC: indeed, when that ministry was merged with Defence Ministry, he – briefly – became the first Pasdaran in charge of the Iranian regular armed forces.

The literal "dot" on the "I" was delivered by the Americans; as the Iraqis mopped up on al-Faw, on 18 April 1988, the US Navy launched its Operation Praying Mantis, aiming to find and sink Iranian Navy warships involved in attacks on international merchant shipping in the lower Persian Gulf. In the course of two naval actions, two Iranian warships were sunk and a third crippled, and Tehran received a strong lesson in modern warfare. Overall, the Operations Ramadan Mubarak and Praying Mantis isolated Iran on the international scene, while greatly boosting not only Iraqi, but also Saudi Arabian and Kuwaiti confidence. On 27 April 1988, Riyadh cut diplomatic links with Tehran, allegedly over the Iranian refusal to limit the number of pilgrims for the Hajj from 155,000 to 45,000.[181]

Chapter 3 notes

147 Lessons p.329 & Ward pp.286-287.
148 Bulloch & Morris pp. 241-243; 'Growing indications of another Basra offensive', *Jane's Defence Weekly*, 10 October 1987 & 'Iran masses troops for major offensive in Gulf', *Jane's Defence Weekly*, 28 November 1987.
149 Murray & Wood p.321
150 For Ramadan Mubarak see Bulloch & Morris pp. 241-243; Cooper & Bishop pp.266-267; Farrokh pp.405-406; Hiro pp. 203-204; Al-Khazraji Muthakerat Muqatel pp.475-514 (hereafter Khazraji); Lessons pp. 373-375; Makki Maarik Al Tahrir Al Kubra Al Iraqiya pp. 231-286 (hereafter Makki); Malovany pp. 399-423; Marashi and Salama p.171; Murray & Woods pp.319-322; Pelletiere pp. 141-142; Pollack 224-225; Ward pp.292-293. FBIS-NES-93-074. See also an article in the Iraqi Armed Forces web site from 27 February-30 August 2013 by Major General Fawzi Berzinji who commanded 19th Infantry Brigade during the offensive.
151 The Raphael-TH pods were delivered to the French Air Force in late 1986 and to the IrAF early in 1988 with Mirage F.1EQ-6s. Information from Tom Cooper, August 26 2016. Based upon Sadik & Cooper, Iraqi Fighters pp. 81-82, 99, 101 For the re-organisation of the IrAF see Cooper & Bishop pp.212-213. Only 19 COR pods were produced by Dassault Aviation.
152 Murray & Woods p.325
153 FBIS-NES-93-074 Part 1, April 19, 1993
154 See Volume 2 pp.61-62 for a more detailed description.
155 For the Iraqi Navy in the invasion of Kuwait and in 1991, when Allied forces sank IrN *Nouh* and *Atika*, see Woods, Mother of all Battles pp.73-78.
156 NTC p.149
157 Op-cit p.145
158 Woods et al, Saddam's Generals pp. 22, 99-100 (hereafter, Saddam's Generals). Khudayyir had distinguished himself as 8th Infantry Division's commander during Karbala-5 and had been given the armoured division as a reward.
159 The Guards commando brigades appear to have remained in the north.
160 FBIS-NES-93-075
161 The 'Tawakkalna ala Allah' Republican Guards Armoured Division appears to have remained as strategic reserve during this operation and the May 1988 offensive.
162 Strengths are based upon the order-of-battle and DDB-2680-103-88 p14.
163 SH-GMID-D-000-529. Najaf Ashraf Division arrived early in 1988 as part of the 'reinforcement' mixed with the bluff of acting as a diversion with the necessity of reinforcing the garrison (P. P., veteran of Ramadan Armoured Brigade, IRGC, interview by Tom Cooper, December 2005)
164 Cordsman p.373
165 Lessons pp 406 f/n 34 & JDW Mobilisation.
166 It is possible that the attack on the northern bridges was made by the 200 Iraqi Navy SEALs mentioned in Saddam's Generals p.177. Account of the air strike on the southern bridge was provided by Brigadier-General Ahmad Sadik, interview to Tom Cooper, October 2007.
167 Meteorological data from nearby Kuwait on Freemeteo web site. The SS-30 vehicle fired 32 127mm rockets with high-explosive warheads up to 30 kilometres far.
168 Javed Ali article p.51
169 For more details of Iraq's chemical weapons programme see CIA-DOC_00010797.pdf, CIA-DOC_ 0000072254.pdf; CIA-RDP90T01298R000300670001-8; 'How Saddam kept deadly gas secret', *The Independent*, 3 July 1998
170 Buchan p.371; Razoux p.441 based on interview with Iraqi medical officer; Saddam's Generals p.48; Javed Ali article pp.49-51. General Makki, who has researched the 1988 offensives for his in-depth history, dismisses this claim.
171 Javed Ali article p.49. Overall sortie data for IrAF and IrAAC as provided by General Makki. Earlier Iraqi reports (see Cooper & Bishop p. 266) cited a total of 318 sorties by both services. Total IrAF commitment to the operation was 12 squadrons: 6 with fighter-bombers, two with bombers, three reconnaissance and one electronic warfare. The Air Defence Command provided three fighter-interceptor squadrons.
172 NTC p.150
173 Ibid, pp.147 & 151
174 It appears that advanced parties of both brigades had established forward bases on Kuwait's Bubiyan Island – with Kuwait's agreement (FBIS-NES-93-074).
175 By 1993, the dismissed brigade commander became a senior

military leader in the Dawah Party, possibly their army Chief-of-Staff.
176 Bulloch & Morris p.242; Lessons p.374.
177 Saddam's Generals p.49
178 For naval operations see Saddam's Generals p.177
179 Saddam's Generals p.16. Lieutenant-General Abid Mohammed al-Kabi, former commander of the Iraqi Navy (1982-1987), interview with Ted Hooton, May 2017.
180 Hiro p.203; Bulloch & Morris p.244. Born in Qom, Shahbazi entered the staff college at the age of 22 and at the time of the revolution was a junior staff officer. He had very close links to the Pasdaran and was regarded as a Khomeini-loyalist.
181 For details on 'Praying Mantis' see Cooper & Bishop pp.267-273, 278-279 f/n 430-433; Farrokh pp.406-408;.Lessons pp.375-381, and Hiro p.236.

4
IRANIAN BURN-OUT

Both sides recognised that the Faw offensive had created a seismic change in fortunes, and a delighted Saddam authorised preparations for a new offensive from the Fish Lake Line; although he reluctantly accepted it would need a month's preparation.

For Iran's SOHQ the loss of the peninsula was especially alarming because it was soon obvious it would face a major new blow which it had little chance of warding off. Opposite the northern end of the Fish Lake Line there remained a flooded area fed by the waters of the Hawizah Marshes, and controlled by the River Arayedh which ran southeast from its southern point into the Karun watershed. This shielded the northern part of SOHQ's front but 'Karbala-8' had left the Pasdaran in the southern part holding a salient, like a chicken awaiting the axe, with the tip of this salient projecting beyond the southern edge of the Fish Lake into the enemy lines. This tip was exposed to fire not only from an arc around the western edge of the salient but also, like the rest of the salient, from across the Shatt. The experience of the Faw Peninsula had demonstrated that this fire against the forward defences would be overwhelming.

Shifting the Schwerpunkt

If Iran was to retain its bridgehead within southern Iraq, this tip of the salient had to be either abandoned completely or held as a lightly-manned breakwater whose garrison would be adequate to prevent its loss to a surprise attack. The clerics in Tehran, and the Pasdaran political allies, obstinately refused to do either and insisted instead the salient be held in force: the Shia martyrdom ethic ensured it would be a huge tomb. Behind the berm-lined salient were a succession of small rivers on whose eastern bank the defenders had raised more berms to replace the levelled Iraqi ones on the western side. SOHQ's only hope was the defensive system between the Rivers Jasim and al-Duaiji – which ran 5 kilometres from the southern edge of the Fish Lake to the Shatt – to provide the illusion of defence in depth. This could be approached through ground usually flooded and always covered in dense barbed wire entanglements and minefields.[182]

The berms were supplemented by trenches and dug-outs and linked by an extensive network of communication trenches, but the whole defensive system was only a kilometre or two deep. It could not be outflanked due to Iraqi-made inundations coming from the southern part of the Fish Lake and stretching to, and across, the international border. However, this flooded area also restricted access to the defences to the ground around Basra-Khorramshahr highway, which could be interdicted by artillery from across the Shatt. To the north lay the impregnable Iraqi defences, the double line of battalion strongpoints which acted like a balcony facing more berm lines, studded with ramps for MBTs, beyond which the

One of a few 155mm M109 howitzers still operated by the 33rd Artillery Group IRIA as of 1987-1988. (E. S. Collection)

Table 5: Order of Battle for Operation Tawakkalna ala Allah (1), May 1988		
Corps	Division	Brigades
Iraq		
Republican Guards Corps	Corps Troops incl. Republican Guards Corps Artillery Brigade	
	Hammurabi Armoured Division Republican Guards	8th & 17th Armoured, 15th Mechanised, 12th Commando Brigades Guards Corps
	Medina Manarwah Armoured Division Republican Guards	2nd & 10th Armoured, 14th Guards Mechanised, 21st Commando Brigades Guards Corps
	Baghdad Infantry Division Republican Guards	4th, 5th, 6th, 7th Infantry, 11th Commando, 16th Special Forces Brigades Guards Corps
	Nebuchadnezzar Infantry Division Republican Guards	19th, 20th, 23rd Infantry Brigades Guards Corps
	Special Purposes Division Republican Guards	3rd Special Forces, 22nd Infantry, and 26th Naval Brigade Guards Corps
III Corps	Corps Troops, 1st & 2nd Commando Brigades of III Corps; III Corps Artillery Brigade	
	3rd Armoured Division	6th & 12th Armoured, 8th Mechanised Brigades
	5th Mechanised Division	26th Armoured, 15th & 20th Mechanised, 65th & 66th Special Forces Brigades
	8th Infantry Division	22nd, 28th, 48th, 429th Infantry Brigades
	11th Infantry Division	23rd, 45th, 47th, 501st Infantry Brigades
	3rd IrAAC Wing	
Iran		
Task Force Karbala	92nd Armoured Division IRIA	3 brigades
	21st Infantry Division IRIA	3 brigades
	8th Val-Fajr Division IRGC	3 brigades
	12th Qa'em-e Mohammad Mechanised Division IRGC	3 brigades
	14th Imam Hossein Division IRGC	3 brigades
	30th Beit-ol-Moghaddas Armoured Division IRGC	1 mechanised brigade
	64th Suduqu Infantry Brigade IRGC	
	84th Zafar Mechanised Brigade IRGC	
	163rd Fateme-ye Zahra Infantry Brigade IRGC	
	33rd Artillery Group IRIA	
	90th Khatam al-Anbiya Artillery Brigade IRGC	
	91st Hadid Artillery Brigade IRGC	
	94th Sha'ban Air Defence Brigade IRGC	
	98th Sahib az-Zaman Engineer Division IRGC	40th and 43rd Engineer Brigades IRGC
	102nd Ba'athat Chemical Decontamination Brigade IRGC	
	2nd Combat Support Group IRIAA	

attacker could strike westwards across firm ground which was ideal for armoured and mechanised forces.

Manning these defences was more difficult because from mid 1987, 11 of the 19 Pasdaran divisions used in the Karbala offensives, together with 18th al-Ghadir Infantry Brigade – a total of 80,000 men – had been sent north for Valfajr-10 around Halabja.[183] Nor was the defence helped by a 10-day amphibious exercise codenamed 'Zulfikar-3' (the sword of the Iman Ali), which had begun on 21 May, to demonstrate that Iran remained a significant naval power – but involved an airborne brigade and other troops who might have acted as a reserve, and elements of the dwindling IRIAF.

Controlled by the headquarters of the Task Force Karbala, the defences consisted of two IRIA divisions (see Table 5 for order of battle), with three divisions and three brigades of Pasdaran.[184] Facing III Corps were 2nd Brigade/21st Infantry Division IRIA and 12th 'Qa'em-e Mohamad' Mechanised Division IRGC, and the reinforced 3rd Brigade/92nd Division, while facing the Guards was the 14th 'Imam Hossein' Division and a mechanised brigade of 30th 'Beit-ol-Moghaddas' Division, reinforced by elements of two Pasdaran infantry brigades. The Iranians had two infantry battalions in the salient, seven on the River Jassim and another seven on River Duaiji. In the rear, straggling across the border, were two Pasdaran infantry brigades (minus battalions with 'Imam Hossein') and a mechanised Brigade of the IRGC. The remainder of Iranian forces in this area consisted of two formations: the 1st Brigade/92nd Division (which was on the border around Shalamcheh with the remainder of 'Beit-ol-Moghaddas'), and the battered 8th 'Val-Fajr' Division IRGC, still recovering from the hammering on the Faw Peninsula. Other infantry elements totalled about 10 battalions. These forces were supported by three IRIA and Pasdaran artillery groups – including a battalion of Brazilian Astros MLRS – with a total of 130 guns (30 self-propelled), and some 50 MLRS augmented by six heavy mortar batteries. The air defence brigade had several batteries of 30mm guns; there was a substantial engineer force of 20,000 men; and a Pasdaran chemical decontamination brigade brought the total strength to 90,000. A total of about 280 MBTs was available, about half of which were serviceable, but the poorly-trained Pasdaran crews would be no match for Iraqi armoured brigades.

Operation 'Tawakkalna ala Allah (1)'

The Iraqi staff, therefore, could be confident of success as they began planning what became Operation Tawakkalna ala Allah.[185] As with 'Ramadan Mubarak' initial planning was conducted by the local command, with Lieutenant-General Salah Aboud Mahmoud's (Aboud) III Corps given the go-ahead on 30 April to eliminate the threat which had been aimed at Basra for the past six years. Even as the last Iranian stragglers on the Faw Peninsula were being rounded up Aboud took the first steps by ordering the northern part of the Fish Lake to be drained dry.[186]

The planners could be fairly certain of favourable weather, indeed after April 26 there was no significant rain in the region and the temperature steadily rose from the mid 30s Centigrade at the beginning of May to the 40s by the middle of the month.[187] Together with the Iranian-built Muqdad Canal, designed to drain the Fish Lake and the former inundated areas to the southeast, the former Karbala-5 battlefield and Iranian territory to the east was dried up and much became a mine-ridden man-made wilderness of rusting barbed wire entanglements on metal posts. It also made it easier to move the mechanised formations in which Iraq had absolute superiority: the area east of the Lake is flat and dusty. The sun posed a logistical problem for both sides as high salinity levels in the ground water meant large amounts of potable water had to be shipped in.

Aboud had had two armoured, two mechanised and seven infantry divisions, but needed a mechanised and five infantry divisions to garrison the strong points to secure the flanks and the jump-off positions. His plan was based upon a frontal assault spearheaded by Rawi's Guards Corps which would strike along the Basra-Khorramshahr highway to take Shalamcheh as well as Twaila Island on the northern Shatt. His corps would strike eastwards towards the Ahvaz-Khorramshahr road shielding Rawi's northern flank from the enemy around the Zayed (also Zaid or Zayd) Salient. Work progressed rapidly, possibly based upon a III Corps contingency plan, and by 10 May Saddam could issue a directive setting Y-Day for 1 June.[188]

Five Guards divisions, with some 70,000 men, left the Faw Peninsula and assembled east of Basra between 10-17 May (for complete order of battle during this operation, see Table 5), while Rawi's staff began detailed planning. He had two armoured, one infantry and one special forces divisions, which had all been 'blooded' on the Faw Peninsula. Correspondingly, he decided to deploy the full force: Rawi's attack would begin on a two-division, 11-brigade, front. Medina (reinforced by 12th Republican Guards Commando Brigade) would strike the salient on his right while Baghdad (reinforced by 16th Republican Guards Special Forces Brigade) on the left would cross the southern Fish Lake. Once they had broken through, Hammurabi would exploit the success with 17th Republican Guards Armoured and 15th Republican Guards Mechanised Brigades. Khalil's Nebuchadnezzar Republican Guards Infantry Division would again act as reserve while Mustafa Hanoush's 26th Republican Guards Naval Commando Brigade would spearhead an amphibious operation to regain Twaila Islands – with commandos and infantry units including Khalil's 22nd Republican Guards Infantry Brigade.

Aboud's plan was based upon a similar two-pronged attack organised into three-phases, using two battle-hardened divisions with 11 brigades. In the first phase a commando and an infantry brigade would cross the drained Fish Lake and establish a bridgehead from which Mahmoud Faizy would then launch his two mechanised brigades in echelon to sweep eastward to the frontier, eventually stopping on the middle River Arayedh. On the left, Tahir, reinforced by one of Mahmoud Faizy's mechanised brigades, would also establish a bridgehead on the eastern bank of the Fish Lake using an infantry brigade of 8th Infantry Division; from this an armoured and a mechanised brigade would sweep through the area north of the Muqdad Canal to the frontier in the second phase. The success would be consolidated by eight brigades of the 8th Infantry Division and the 11th Infantry Division under Brigadiers Natiq Shaker and Sami Abbas respectively; Mahmoud Faizy and Tahir would establish a covering bridgehead in Iran as far east as Shalamcheh in the third phase using the River Arayedh to shield his left.

The Iraqis had only 20 days to transfer troops and equipment, expand ammunition and supply dumps, prepare for the amphibious assault and ensure detailed reconnaissance of the enemy positions. Aboud had to organise much of the preparatory work including new approach roads to the western bank of the Fish Lake, firing positions for two tank battalions of 8th and 11th Infantry Divisions (for direct fire support) and strong points so that armoured and mechanised brigades could do the same. The staffs made extensive use of sand-tray models to plan their operations and to brief subordinates while each corps created a full-scale replica of the defences upon which the troops could practise their assault both day and night.

Advance by Fire

The assault force consisted of 136,500 men with 680 MBTs, supported by a powerful artillery train.[189] Aboud would be supported by 25 artillery battalions (450 tubes), including two MLRS battalions (36 BM-21 each with 40 tubes) and 12 heavy mortar batteries (72 120mm mortars), and two regiments of FROG surface-to-surface missiles. Aboud augmented this fire power by re-organising the brigade mortar companies into Mortar Nodes, deployed some 200 metres apart. These 750 82mm tubes on a four-kilometre front received 200 bombs per platoon for this task, and were to provide support for the assault troops for 45 minutes just before S-Hour. Afterwards, they were to fire into the enemy rear until the infantry had taken the positions whereupon they would rejoin their brigades. Rawi's troops would be supported by 28 artillery battalions (504 tubes), some firing from across the Shatt, including some MLRS batteries and a FROG battalion, although the Astros batteries were not used because they had expended almost all their ammunition.

Furthermore, each corps had two organic engineer battalions and each division had an engineer battalion, while Rawi also received an extra bridging battalion and, like the Iranians in the Hawizah Marshes, sections of foam were available to create lightweight bridges. The amphibious assault would use 134 fibreglass- and metal boats, capable of carrying some 1,350 men, 55 rubber dinghies carrying 350 men, and would be supported by 11 GSP ferries and 12 PTS amphibious transporters. There would again be extensive use of chemical weapons and each corps had a chemical defence company with Soviet DDA-53 or DDA-66 decontamination trucks for clothing, ARS-12 or ARS-14 area decontamination vehicles and BRDM-2RKh chemical reconnaissance vehicles.[190]

The offensive was preceded in early May by intense aerial preparation: after deploying two wings with 60 fighter-bombers at al-Kut and Ali Ibn Abu Talib ABs, the IrAF flew 308 attack sorties on 24 May 1988 alone – which the IRIAF could counter with only about a dozen.

Maskirovka

These attacks and obvious enemy preparations meant the Iranians could view the coming days with foreboding. However, they were uncertain whether or not the enemy meant to strike east towards the border or north into the Hawizah Marshes. To increase their confusion the Iraqi Army staff staged diversions on other fronts, while Saddam brought Y-Day forward to 26 May 1988, and pushed S-Hour back three hours from the usual 06:30 to 09:30, by which time the enemy would have stood down with many men assigned to work parties. The spur-of-the-moment decision was apparently because he had convinced himself the enemy had divined his plans after SIGINT reported plans to reinforce the southern positions.[191] (10).

Saddam managed to confuse not only the enemy but his own generals too. In the early afternoon of 24 May Rawi was summoned

Operation Tawakkalna ala Allah (1) saw the first combat deployment of the Sukhoi Su-25 in the environment for which this type was originally designed: provision of close air support for conventional mechanised formations on the advance. This Iraqi Su-25 was narrowly missed by an Iranian MANPAD. (Farzin Nadimi Collection)

to a meeting of the Advanced General Command Headquarters to discuss final arrangements. Then, at 20:00 Operations Chief Hussein Rashid and Planning Chief Qader flew in by helicopter from Baghdad to inform him that Saddam had decided to change the

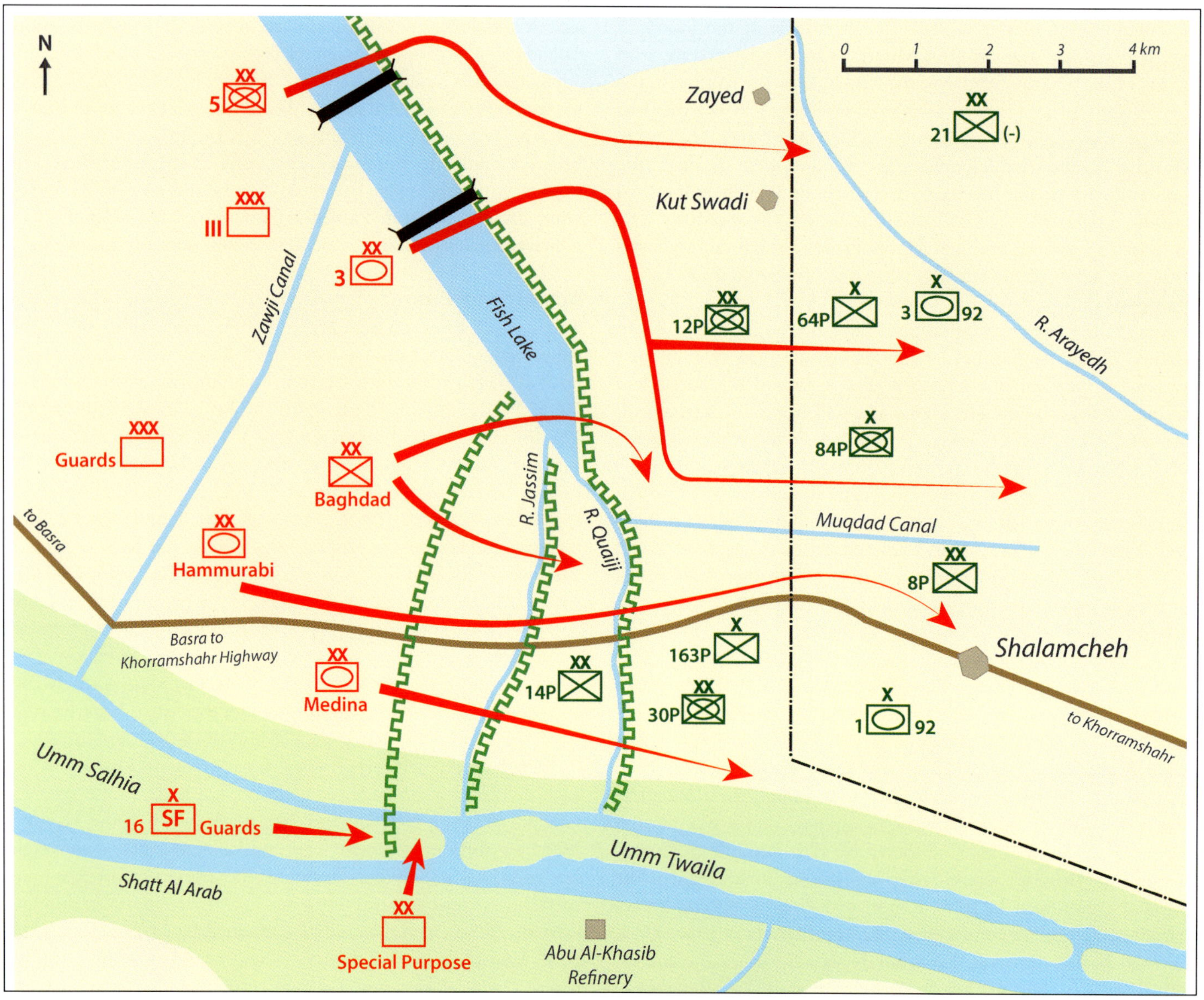

Map 4: The Operation Tawakkalna ala Allah

4 IRANIAN BURN-OUT

Iranian troops scrambling for cover, as medics run to assist the injured, while their positions are blanketed by Iraqi artillery fire. (Farzin Nadimi Collection)

As usual during the later stages of the Iran-Iraq War, the Iraqi artillery played a dominant role in the Operation Tawakkalna ala Allah. The crew of this gun was photographed just seconds before opening fire. (Albert Grandolini Collection)

timings. Aboud was not informed until 01:00 on 25 May, although he may have had a hint earlier because during the afternoon he ordered the 3rd IrAAC Wing to intensify reconnaissance.

Despite the last-minute chaos, the bombardment began on schedule at 09:30 on 25 May and achieved total surprise. The IrAF and the IrAAC began striking behind the lines, the former deploying large numbers of brand-new Sukhoi Su-25K ground-attack aircraft for the first time. The bombardment was controlled by the corps artillery brigades with a dedicated communications network extending down to forward observers at company level. At corps and division level were gun battalions, some with ballistic computers to help make rapid adjustments in targeting or weight of fire, as well as MLRS battalions all ready to provide general fire support.

In its initial bombardment the artillery sought to saturate Iranian headquarters, command posts (from battalion to division level), artillery- and air defence positions, and engineer units, while MLRS also targeted supply dumps, communication choke points and operational level reserves. Multiple FROG missiles were fired at key enemy headquarters. This barrage of high-intensity was maintained until the assault units crossed their jump-off lines and began sweeping into the enemy rear to disrupt the movement of reserves.[192]

While the operational-level onslaught was already going on, artillery battalions assigned to specific brigades opened fire at Iranian anti-armour positions and observation posts, tank and mortar positions, minefields, and reserves. Once all targets had been engaged the brigade commander authorized support of neighbouring units. The Iraqi gunners had grown in skill in delivering massive fire, in counter-battery capabilities and in shifting fire. By contrast only the IRIA possessed the skills for these tasks but lacked the materials, while Iranian target acquisition and attack had been eroded and often relied upon 'blind fire' techniques or striking potential targets selected from a map.[193]

Infantry Leading

Exposed to the hail of fire, the Iranians sought cover in their trenches, fox-holes and dug-outs. Before long, an ominous melon smell warned them of chemical weapons, including nerve agents, which the Iraqis used extensively. Forward positions were hit by cyanide and nerve agents that worked quickly – but dispersed quickly too. Rear areas were hit by slower-dispersing mustard gas to prevent the enemy forming up for a counter-attack. Most of the chemicals were delivered by BM-21s (their warheads contained a small amount of explosive and three plastic bottles containing 8-12 kilograms of chemical agents that could be mixed and matched). Sarin ('Agent GB') was delivered by 120mm mortars, but also by artillery pieces of 130mm, 152mm, and 155mm calibre; 130mm and 155mm artillery shells were used to deploy mustard gas; while Agent GF was delivered by 152mm and 155mm shells. Under threat, the Iranians scrambled to use their atropine injectors and donned gas masks, but with temperatures reaching up to 41°C, these proved too hot to war for any length of time.

Meanwhile, Iraqi mine-clearing teams – deployed already the previous evening – were clearing lanes for the infantry, enabling

Dry season and Iraqi shelling covered most of the battlefield with immense clouds of dust and smoke, helping to conceal, in this photograph, an advancing Iraqi infantry assault. (Farzin Nadimi Collection)

Fire-action by an Iranian 175mm M107 self-propelled howitzer. By 1988, far too few of such artillery pieces were left in operational condition to match the Iraqi artillery. (via E. S.)

of destroying MBTs which proved very robust: already the October 1973 Arab-Israeli War demonstrated that success depended less upon accuracy and more upon high rates of fire. Iranian ground-based TOW teams often had to spend four missiles to destroy a tank; Iraqi teams regularly required 6-8 Milan or HOTs, while teams equipped with Soviet-made AT-3 Saggers required up to 30 missiles for one kill.[194] To decrease this threat, the Iraqis let their infantry and commandos lead the attack with MBTs and IFVs providing fire-support from the flank and the rear.

Intensive bombardment raised immense clouds of smoke and dust. These were further enhanced by smoke screens to conceal the infantry while this was advancing through the wire and over the berms, and began destroying forward Iranian positions.[195]

In the north, infantry of the III Corps required 30 minutes to cross the Fish Lake and establish bridgeheads around the exits of two causeways. Both were then reinforced by GSP ferries, before the engineers threw bridges across the lake and started clearing obstacles to allow the armoured forces to cross with little incident, regroup on the eastern side of the lake and push towards the frontier. Mahmoud Faizy drove south-eastwards while Tahir helped to clear the eastern bank and then pushed into the Pentangle both to threaten the Diaiji defences and to support Sattar's Hammurabi Division.

Hammash's Medina Division found most of the defenders of the salient dead or stunned, and thus quickly swept south of the Fish Lake to take the Jassim defences by 10:42; while Sattar's Hammurabi Division was brought up and by 11:07 its 17th Republican Guards Armoured Brigade had punched a 500-metre breach through the enemy lines. At 12:50 the Baghdad and Medina Divisions began to push into the Duaiji defences while Sattar pressed on and broke through the last defensive system at 13:25. He then drove to the border and joined Tahir to envelop

rifle units to move forward, followed by engineers that widened the lanes for tanks. Medina Division advanced in battalion-sized, all-armoured battlegroups which included mine-clearing tanks and AVBLs. The threat to the armoured fists from anti-armour missiles remained a concern and they had top priority for direct-support fire. However, the missile threat was mitigated by the difficulties

4 IRANIAN BURN-OUT

A still from a video showing a T-72 of the Republican Guard advancing during the Operation Tawakkalna ala Allah (1). (Tom Cooper Collection)

T-72s represented the backbone of armoured units of the Republican Guards, and led most of its offensives in 1988. This example was captured on a video during advance on Shalamcheh. (Tom Cooper Collection)

the enemy in between. The dry ground, and a considerable dose of professionalism in combined-arms operations, enabled the Iraqis to advance fast, although – reportedly – at least one Iraqi armoured unit ran into major problems while advancing without adequate infantry support.[196]

Pasdaran on the Run

The Iranians initially fought well, inflicted 'significant' casualties, and even launched several counter-attacks and took some prisoners. However, the Iraqis reacted by additional artillery barrages and emergency CAS provided by helicopters, quickly suppressing most resistance. Therefore, only one of the Iranian counter-attacks north of the formerly inundated area briefly halted the Iraqis before the IRGC started to crack: artillery barrages and chemical weapons had killed or incapacitated many of the defenders, and demoralized the rest. Attempts at a fighting retreat thus quickly dissolved into a rout, during which Pasdaran commanders showed a great predilection to commandeer vehicles and speed their way to safety.

With the defence dissolving Tahir and Sattar pushed eastwards to the frontier, which they crossed at 14:45, then went on to take the Iranian border town of Shalamcheh. However, when Hammurabi pushed reconnaissance forces beyond the frontier towards Khorramshahr fierce resistance forced them to return.

Meanwhile, the Medina's 16th Special Forces Brigade of the Republican Guards worked its way along the Shatt's northern islands to take Twaila Island, while SEALS from the 26th Naval Commando Brigade Republican Guards secured bridgeheads. Reinforcements were initially ferried across the Shatt by boats and barges, some carrying MBTs and APCs, until engineers threw a pontoon bridge by 15:00. Supported by the 16th and 22nd Brigades of the Republican Guards, the naval commandos quickly overwhelmed the defenders and by 18:00 all the islands had been recaptured to conclude 'Tawakalna ala Allah' – within just 8.5 hours instead of the anticipated 28. Iraqi casualties remain uncertain but probably included no more than 3,000, although they certainly suffered significant material losses; one of US military attache that witnessed this operation from the rear counted about 70 knocked-out Iraqi AFVs, including T-72 MBTs, being towed to the rear after the offensive.[197]

The offensive was a disaster for Iran, the military of which lost up to 10% of its heavy equipment – including about 100 MBTs and 150 guns. However, Iraqi claims of inflicting 400,000 casualties were wildly exaggerated: the actual figure was closer to about 6,000,

The massive Iraqi deployment of chemical weapons resulted in heavy casualties for Pasdaran and Basiji units in 1986-1988. This in turn caused the recruitment of Iranian volunteers to drop by 70%, denying the IRGC even the ability to provide effective defences on the southern front. This photograph shows a captured Iraqi T-55 being used by Iranian clergy during one of the recruiting drives. (Photo by Mamhoud-Reza Kalari)

An AH-1J passing low over Iranian positions in Shalamcheh area, in May 1988. (Albert Grandolini Collection)

including a few prisoners.

Khomeini remained defiant. On 28 May 1988, he addressed the new Majlis (elected on 8 April) and appealed to his troops stating their losses did not matter for when they

'…began treading this holy path, they have lost nothing to be worried about, nor have they suffered any loss of which they should repent…. The outcome of the Iraq-imposed war will be determined

Jeep-mounted 106mm M40 recoilless guns were often the only means of fire-support for lightly-armed Pasdaran and Basiji. (Photo by E. S.)

on the battlefields, not through negotiations.'[198]

Nevertheless, damage was already caused. Recruiting reportedly dropped by 70%, and there were protest rallies which the IRGC had to suppress. Eventually, even Khomenei was forced to recognize that the war was lost and a political solution inevitable. In this regard, he feared the reaction of the Pasdaran and hard-line clerics, and thus needed a lightening rod: as Khomeini's representative in the SDC, Rafsanjani had been 'de-facto commander-in-chief', but on 2 June 1988, Khomeini ratified this formally, appointing him officially as the commander-in-chief of all Iranian armed forces. However, the terminally ill Ayatollah was so much out of touch with reality, that he demanded Rafsanjani to end the war by military means within six months.

Even if unaware of there being no chance of an Iranian victory before this appointment, Rafsanjani was no fool. As soon as he learned the truth, he concluded that his primary task would be to persuade Khomeini to accept a diplomatic solution. In the meantime, he publicly recognized that it would take three or four months to re-organise and regroup Iranian forces, and created a unified command under his supervision. While considering, but rejecting, a plan to merge the IRIA with the IRGC, he was able to sideline Rezai – with help from Shabazi, who was not only a fully-trained staff officer, but also a staunch Khomeini-loyalist with close links to the IRGC.[199]

Recovering the Majnoons

With everybody in Tehran knowing that Khomeini was about to die, most of top Iranian clergy and politicians began jockeying for position, and nobody was eager to become associated with another bloody (and ultimately futile) offensive. The only area where Iran was still able to exercise pressure upon Iraq was in the north. Correspondingly, the JCS assembled four IRIA- and 15 IRGC-divisions, together with 17 brigades of Pasdaran and Basiji – total of some 220,000 men – between Mahabad and Kermanshah.[200]

Iraqis recognized this threat and a concern over the northern front was clearly expressed when Saddam chaired a meeting of the AFGC on 26 May 1988. Chief-of-Staff Khazraji and his Operations Chief, Hussain Rashid, were especially worried that only half of Iraq's infantry – 64 brigades (including commandos) – were with I and V Corps in the north. Both corps commanders were seeking reinforcements, including up to three Guards divisions, but Saddam was reluctant to strip the southern front.[201] On the other side, he was surprised at the enemy staff's failure to transfer troops from the north to the south along Iran's poor railroad network, while optimistic about the prospect of defensive operations in the north, and concluded that the dispatch of four or eight divisions would be no guarantee for a major success. Commenting that this would force the southern front upon defensive, and anxious to exploit the success of Operations Ramadan Mubarak and Tawakkalna alla Allah, Saddam concluded that striking in the Majnoon islands was a preferable option.[202] Hussein Rashid agreed with this idea, commenting that the VI Corps – then under Major General Yaljin Omar Adil – had already drafted a plan for securing South Majnoon but had been told to wait until the northern front had settled down.[203]

Khairallah fully supported a follow-on attack upon North Majnoon, but he did not anticipate it would be practical for another three months. Inpatient, Saddam then ordered IV, VI, and III Corps, and the Republican Guards to retake the islands, while the I Special

An RPG-team of the IRGC in action against advancing Iraqis. (Farzin Nadimi Collection)

Corps was to launch a diversion on the central front.

Hussein Rashid was enthusiastic, especially as work on draining the Hawizah Marshes meant armour could be moved further forward. Moreover, the enemy had withdrawn their artillery from the Majnoon islands and all thought that Shabazi's inexperience would help exploit recent successes.[204]

On 1 June 1988, AFGC met again and the corps commanders were informed the next offensive would be to recover the Majnoon islands on or about 25 June. The Guards would strike the islands, supported by VI Corps, while III Corps would encircle the enemy east of the marshes. Anticipating the war to last for another 18 months, on 5 June 1988 Saddam wrote to Khazraji, advising him that the decision had been made to go-ahead with the Majnoon offensive so that Iraq could exploit its recent successes before the enemy could interfere. He demanded intensified reconnaissance and a comprehensive electronic warfare plan, but would include artillery fire to erode enemy strength.[205] Detailed planning for what became Operation 'Tawakkalna ala Allah 2' began on 12 June 1988. However, its execution was then disrupted by what became the final Iranian offensive of this war.

Iran's Lame Response: Operation Beit-ol-Mogaddas-7

Rafsanjani's first weeks as Commander-in-Chief of the Islamic Republic's armed forces were a nightmare, for his troops faced a trial as terrible as that of September 1980. Indeed, the fear that those events would be repeated was omnipresent in the minds of many civilian and military leaders in Tehran.

The southern front was in the biggest crisis since the heady days of 1982, with powerful, combat-hardened Iraqi forces now poised to drive deep into the Khuzestan province. The defenders were battered and demoralised, and lacking troops and equipment. Realising the strategic peril, Rafsanjani authorised the stripping of the northern front and about a dozen divisions had begun the long, slow, trip; first eastwards to Tehran then southwards over the poor transport network. Even by the end of the Iran-Iraq War, most of units were still in central Iran.

Unable to permit the enemy to threaten oilfields of Khuzestan again, Rafsanjani was enough of a realist to recognise he lacked the material strength to push the Iraqis back to the Fish Lake. Yet, as he observed to a press conference on 14 June 1988, that the enemy had now advanced beyond the Fish Lake Line and was exposed. Reconnaissance by Pasdaran and, probably, IRIA Special Forces showed the armed and mechanised spearhead of 'Tawakkalna ala Allah' had been withdrawn and infantry divisions were throwing up defences along the frontier and around Shalamcheh. Whether or not Rafsanjani knew the Guard Corps was being transferred to the southern banks of the Hawr al Hawizah is unknown, but he did recognize a small window of opportunity had opened to catch the enemy off guard. He hoped to buy time as the Iranian Foreign Ministry sought a diplomatic solution.

'The Homeland is in Danger' was a slogan which many a demoralised military and clerical leader had hoped would spur the demoralized troops to further heroic sacrifice. However, despite the energetic efforts by the imams, the troops were all too well-aware that the war was lost. In addition to Iraqi chemical weapons, morale was also affected by the weather; during May the temperature steadily rose into the mid 40s centigrade, reaching 49° on 13 June. This was especially trying for infantrymen whose canteens held only enough water for a couple of hours and, with fighting likely to take place under a scorching sun, medical advice was being given to prevent the men falling prey to heatstroke, including 'use your

A column of BMP-1s carrying Pasdaran towards the forward operational area, at dusk on 12 June 1988. (Albert Grandolini Collection)

headscarves to prevent direct sunlight on your heads and faces'.[206]

For a fortnight SOHQ frantically re-organised its units and rushed down supplies – together with whatever reinforcements it could lay its hand on – usually in trucks driving through the night without headlights. Some 70 artillery pieces, and few battalions in replacements and reinforcements reached the front, but the IRIAF meanwhile was down to a point where it could only provide eight fighter-bombers and its SAM-sites to provide support.[207]

Ya Aba Abdellah!

The Iranian troops moved out at dusk of 12 June 1988, following receipt of the code-phrase 'Ya Aba Abdellah'. Dubbed Operation Beit al-Moqaddas-7 – in memory of the great victory of April-May 1982 – their assault began at 23.30hrs, with an attempt by four under-strength IRGC divisions and one armoured brigade (some 20,000 troops and 160 MBTs in total) along a 15-kilometre frontline around Kut Swadi. Their assault was supported by 120mm mortars, some 175 artillery tubes, and 22 or 23 attack sorties by the IRIAF.[208]

The area that came under attack was referred to by the CIA as 'The Step': it was occupied by the 8th, 11th, and 19th Infantry Divisions of the Iraqi Army – some 50,000 veterans of defensive successes. These held newly-constructed defences that lacked the depth and the combination of minefields and barbed wire that shielded the Fish Lake defences. There are strong indications that their garrisons had been a 'little lax' following recent victories perhaps even 'demob happy'. Furthermore, it is certain that the Iraqi intelligence failed to obtain enough information to warn the defenders – perhaps because most of the attacking formations relied on landlines and couriers, rather than radio communications.

The first inkling of trouble was a succession of reports from Brigadier Majid Mahmud Hussein's 19th Infantry Division at 21:30 that enemy truck convoys were driving into positions in Iran beyond artillery range. Just 105 minutes later, at 23:15, the short Iranian bombardment began and soon many forward positions of Hussein and his northern neighbour, Brigadier Natiq Shaker's 8th Infantry Division, were overrun. The Pasdaran briefly regained their old offensive spirit to drive 9-10 kilometres into the Iraqi line around Kut Swadi, inflicting heavy casualties – including destruction of 30 MBTs and the capture of about 700 prisoners. However, the Iraqis were not cowed.

III Corps commander Aboud ordered the remaining strongpoints to hold out even if encircled, and quickly alerted his gunners. Although many batteries had been withdrawn for training and had to be ordered to rejoin their units, a mass of artillery units moved to the threatened section of the frontline. One saving grace for the Iraqis was that the northern part of the Fish Lake Line – the double line of strong points – was still manned as a jump-off line for 'Tawakkalna ala Allah 2'. This ensured defence in depth while other units were training around the Fish Lake. Furthermore, assembly of Rawi's corps near the strongpoint line in anticipation of 'Tawakkalna ala Allah 2' meant that first his batteries and then his brigades were available to respond to Baghdad's demand for a counter-offensive.

Iraqi Counterattack
Within hours, Aboud assembled a force of 10 brigades, totalling 45,500 troops and 315 MBTs, including Tahir's 3rd Armoured Division (6th, 12th Armoured, 8th Mechanised Brigade); Mahmoud Faizy's 5th Mechanised Division (26th Armoured, 15th, 20th Mechanised Bdes); and Brigadier Sami Abbas' 11th Infantry Division (23rd, 45th, 47th, 501st Infantry Bdes). These troops were originally to spearhead a counter-offensive he planned to launch at noon. However, his subordinates began launching counter-attacks and contained the threat already by 08:00. Abbas was ordered to use one brigade to reinforce 8th Division's beleaguered strongpoints then struck around Bubyan at 05:00 to begin retaking the lost northern positions, secure the eastern bank of the Fish Lake and allow batteries to deploy there. There was little impediment to Iraqi movement for the IRIAF provided only token support: a lone dawn strike package of eight aircraft with 'iron' bombs was nearly drowned in a combination of about a dozen of Iraqi interceptors and dozens of SAMs. Two aircraft were shot down and two others badly damaged. By contrast, most of the 170 IrAF and 240 IrAAC sorties flown on 13 June encountered next to no resistance from Iranian air defences.

As the counter-attacks were launched, Aboud completed his planning. Tahir would strike across the Fish Lake – as in 'Tawakkalna ala Allah 1' – while Mahmud Faizi would strike eastwards on the southern flank towards Kut Swadi and the Muqdad Canal. Natiq Shaker's 8th Infantry Division (reinforced by Abbas' infantry brigade, 65th SF Brigade and 34th Armoured Brigade from 1st Mechanised Division) was to regain the rest of its lost positions around Bubyan. Khudayyir's 6th Armoured Division and Thamir Sultan's 1st Mechanised Division would remain in reserve. Throughout the morning Iraqi artillery fire pounded the enemy, inflicting heavy casualties on troops who were often in exposed positions in the desert, and Iraqi SIGINT began picking up a growing stream of pleas for supplies and reinforcements.

Aboud arrived at Majid Mahmud Hussein's 19th Division's headquarters to use it as a forward command post. Meanwhile, Saddam arrived at III Corps headquarters at 10:00 – with most of the Iraqi Army's senior command team to look over his shoulder – concerned that the gains of 'Tawakkalna ala Allah' might be lost, and that 'Tawakkalna ala Allah 2', might have to be cancelled. Aboud quickly reassured him and said that the lost ground would be retaken by his counter-offensive which would start in less than two hours. Saddam was not totally convinced and took out insurance by alerting Rawi to be ready to launch a counter-offensive by dusk if Aboud's attack failed.

The Pasdaran were well aware of Aboud's preparations, which were completed by 11:30. One of them, Ahmad Dehqan, wrote in his diary:

Iraqi troops inspecting the bodies of fallen Pasdaran found on one of the Majnoon Islands after these were recaptured. (via S. S.)

I have a bad feeling. I think something bad is going to happen tonight. Everybody shares the same feeling. Qasem has put his head on his knees at a dugout. I want to say something, but change my mind...²⁰⁹

Meanwhile, the IrAF and the IrAAC were roaming the skies: most of the 213 sorties flown by the air force, and 391 by helicopters, between 14 and 15 June 1988 were undertaken over this battlefield. They de-facto blocked any kind of Iranian movement during daylight hours, destroyed vital supplies of ammunition and water, and debilitated the attackers' ability to fight. At 11.30hrs, about 360 Iraqi artillery pieces and 760 mortars opened the preparatory bombardment as the armoured brigades moved out followed by the infantry both in armoured vehicles and on foot. The Iraqis quickly closed with the enemy and there was fierce fighting as the crack-lipped Pasdaran defenders rapidly ran out first of anti-armour missiles and then of RPG rounds. This allowed the tanks and troop carriers to get ever closer and attack from the flanks, gradually – but with increasing speed – pushing the Pasdaran back towards the Iraqi frontier.

By 16.30hrs, it was all over, and the surviving Iranians were back on their start lines.

Guards in the Flank
Meanwhile, the Republican Guards Corps had swung around to face the threat and at 16:30 Rawi's Chief-of-Staff, Ismael, telephoned Aboud to say that the corps was ready to join the advance to the international frontier, and would attack at 17:00. Aboud informed him that his troops were already on the frontier, but that he was willing to withdraw them and allow the Guards to retake the frontier positions provided there was a 30-minute delay so he could withdraw his men and avoid friendly fire.

When Saddam learned of this he was delighted both at the selflessness of the III Corps commander and the close degree of co-operation between the Army and the Guards. He ordered Rawi to place his forces under III Corps – the only occasion ever that the Guards came under Army command. The Guards commander drove to 19th Division headquarters but still sought a role. Aboud tactfully convinced him there was no need and he could return to the reserve. At 18:00 Aboud signed off the counter-offensive and soon received a congratulatory telephone call from Saddam.

Once Beit al-Moqaddas-7 was over, the Iranians talked-up the result claiming to have inflicted 18,000 casualties (the figure was probably 2,500) and taken up to 2,100 prisoners (it was probably less than 1,000) and described it as 'the first sweet fruit' of Rafsanjani's appointment. The new Iranian commander-in-chief exploited the opportunity to claim he planned more extensive operations and appropriate responses to the recent Iraqi successes.²¹⁰ In reality, the Iranians lost about 4,000 troops – or a quarter of their strength – and had achieved nothing except to further weaken their forces. A CIA report from June 18 noted:

'The concentration of (Iraqi) armour in the marsh area is the largest since the battle of Kursk in 1943 between German and Soviet armies. Iraq can launch an offensive at any time; Iranian forces are in a poor position to defend against an attack out of the "step" area particularly if Iraq, as in recent battles, uses extensive artillery and chemical bombardment.'²¹¹

Chapter 4 notes
182 NTC pp.151-153. Heyman article, Advance of the Intelligent Battlefield p.35; DIA Ground Forces Intelligence Study, Iran p.42. Iran acquired some 2.5 million American M-2, M-16A, M-14, M-18A1 anti-personnel and M-15, M-19 and M-21 anti-armour mines between 1969 and 1979, while China, Italy and North Korea supplied both anti-personnel and anti-armour mines.
183 They were identified by Iraqi intelligence as 7th 'Vali Asr', 9th 'Badr',10th 'Seyed o-Shohada', 17th'Ali Ibn Abu-Taleb', 19th 'Fajr', 21st 'Iman Reza', 27th 'Mohamad Rasoolallah', 31st 'Ashura', 32nd 'Ansar al-Hossein', 41st 'Sarallah' and 155th 'Shohada' Divisions. CRRC SH-GMID-D-000-530. In addition the 10th 'Seyed ol-Shohada' Division which participated in the Hawizah Marshes battles was also sent north.
184 This order of battle is based upon Iraqi intelligence.
185 'On God we depend' although it has been translated as 'In God We Trust'. Afterwards it was re-designated as 'Tawakkalna ala Allah 1'.
186 For Tawakkalna ala Allah 1 see Cooper & Bishop pp.273-274; Farrokh pp.408-409; Hiro pp.206-7, 238; Lessons pp. 381-3, 385-6, 407 f/n 58; Khazraji pp.515-536; Makki pp. 287-330; Malovany pp.424-429; Marashi and Salama pp. 171-172; Murray & Woods pp.325-327; Pelletiere pp.142-144; Pollack pp.225-227; Ward p.293.
187 Meteorological data from nearby Kuwait on Freemeteo web site.
188 For his reasoning see CRRC SH-PDWN-D-000-730.
189 Based upon the ORBAT from DIA DDB-2680-103-88 p14.
190 See NTC pp. 164-167 for Iraqi offensive and defensive chemical capabilities.
191 For the last-minute changes see Makki p.294; Murray & Woods p.326. Iranian sources claim IRIAF SIGINT was conducting real-time interceptions of Iraqi Army communications.
192 For Iraqi artillery techniques see NTC pp.115-122
193 Lessons pp.445-447
194 Ibid, p443
195 For Iraqi Army tactics see NTC pp.50, 54-70
196 Lessons p.382
197 Francona, pp27-28
198 Hiro p 207; Lessons p. 383
199 Bulloch & Morris p.244; Hiro, pp207-209
200 JDW, Mobilisation & SH-GMID-D-000-530
201 For these discussions see CRRC SH-PDWN-D-000-730
202 See Volume 1 pp24-25 for a description of the Iranian transport network; Murray & Woods p.320; CRRC SH-PDWN-D-000-730
203 VI Corps had 12th Armoured, 25th, 31st, 32nd and 35th Infantry Divisions.
204 CRRC SH-PDWN-D-000-730
205 CRRC SH-SPPC-D-000-229
206 Mosalla-Nejad pp62 & 67; meteorological data from nearby Kuwait on Freemeteo web site.
207 For Operation 'Beit-ol-Mogaddas 7' see Bishop & Cooper pp.274-275; Farrokh pp.409-410; Hiro pp 207-208, 238; Lessons p.386; Malovany pp.429-430; Makki pp.346-347; Mosalla-Nejad pp.61-70; Pelletiere p.144; CIA National Intelligence Dailies from website foia.cia.gov/browse_docs.asp June 18; 'Iran's assault in Iraq – A morale booster?' *Jane's Defence Weekly*, 25 June 1988 (hereafter JDW Morale Booster.
208 Rafsanjani claimed this offensive involved 50 battalions (25,000) while the Iraqis reportedly engaged 10-12 brigades (40,000). JDW Morale Booster. See also CIA National Intelligence Daily 18 June 1988. All of available Iranian publications are curiously silent about the IRAA's involvement in this operation.
209 Mosalla-Nejad p.67
210 JDW Morale Booster.
211 CIA National Intelligence Daily

5
END GAME

With the Iranian counter-offensive crushed, detailed planning and preparations for 'Tawakkalna ala Allah 2' were renewed on 12 June 1988. They involved only nine meetings, each chaired by Saddam, with the agreed outline developed into detailed plans involving the various commands, the IrAAC, and the air commands, and completed by 15 June.

The objective was to regain the last large bloc of territory still in enemy hands, the economically important Majnoon Islands in the Hawizah Marshes, which one Iraqi journalist described thus 'Vast areas of water stretch as far as the eye can see... recurring dust storms make visibility difficult'.[212]

Waters of the southern marshes were usually one-and-a-half meters deep, while in the north they usually evaporated under the summer sun. The Iranians had created a lake on the eastern edge of the marshes to help flood Iraqi territory and impede an assault upon the Majnoons; while the Iraqis had begun extensive drainage work to reduce the cover provided by the reed banks to enemy operations, and to deprive deserters and their supporters of their marshy sanctuary. They also began digging a drainage ditch, the 30-metre-wide Qutaiba Canal, along the frontier which also augmented III Corps' forward defences and helped to drain the flooded area. However, high levels in the rivers feeding the marshes in 1988 had meant water seeped along the edges of the marshes, leaving a strip of boggy ground some 3.5 kilometres from the edge, to hinder the assembly and movement of armoured/mechanised forces.

Preparing to retake the Majnoons

The Iraqi plan envisaged Rawi's Guards Corps to sweep through the Majnoons from south to north, using powerful artillery preparation and protective fire. It was a difficult task for, despite extensive work to drain the marshes and the summer sun evaporating the waters, the attackers still had to advance across deep, reed-lined and mine-infested waters which required an amphibious element to the assault. This drive would be supported by a heliborne landing of a special forces battalion behind the enemy lines to isolate forward-deployed Iranians and maintain contact with VI Corps (Major General Yaljin Umar Adil). The latter was to strike east from al-Uzayr (also Uzair) for some 15 kilometres to isolate North Majnoon from the north as well as to divert enemy forces. Aboud's III Corps would shield Rawi's right by sweeping northwards from 'The Step' through Talaiyeh (also Shabhabi) and Kushk towards Hoveyzeh and the River Karun to prevent intervention by enemy forces around Ahvaz and Khorramshahr.[213]

Rawi's Republican Guards totalled about 61,000 men (see Table 6 for order of battle) in 13 brigades controlled by the Hammurabi Republican Guards Armoured Division, Medina Republican Guards Armoured Division, Baghdad Republican Guards Infantry Division, and Mustafa Hanoush's Guards Special Forces Division (with elements of the Nebucadnezar Republican Guards Infantry Division). While part of the assault would come from the Ghuzail – the exposed salt flats north of the Fish Lake strongpoint line, along the strip linking South Majnoon – most of it would be through, or over, the marshes. Once the island was secure a similar assault would be made upon North Majnoon. They would be supported in the west by VI Corps, with 18,000 men in six brigades under the control of the 25th Infantry Division.[214]

Rawi would be covered by Aboud's III Corps with 61,500 men, leaving 8th and 19th Infantry Divisions to cover the frontier, and strike northwest from 'The Step' with Thamir Sultan's 1st and Mahmud Faizi's 5th Mechanised Divisions, Tahir's 3rd Armoured Division and 6th Armoured Division (now under Brigadier Hussein Hassan Adday) and 41st Infantry Division. The original plan called for two brigades (infantry and commando) supported by an armoured brigade to establish a bridgehead where 'The Step' turned northward. This would be exploited by an under-strength armoured division and a mechanised division to drive 30 kilometres through Kushk to cut the Kushk-Jeghir ('Jofeyr') road and to seal the eastern bank of the marshes. The two divisions would then push beyond Jeghir and occupy ground to the east, to seize enemy supply dumps, while the mechanised division would send its armoured brigade to seize the eastern end of the Kheiber Bridge (see Volume 2) which led to North Majnoon.

The assault force thus consisted of a nominal 140,000 men with 850 MBT, but due to the continuance of generous leave entitlements it was probably 126,000 men and 750 MBT. Its artillery train was remarkable: it consisted of 39 field and medium battalions (702 guns), an MLRS battalion (18 pieces), 16 heavy mortar batteries and two FROG battalions with the 225th Missile Brigade headquarters. The

Iraqi troops resting after bringing one of their Czechoslovak-made OT-62 APCs into a starting position for next offensive towards the end of the war with Iran. (Albert Grandolini Collection)

Table 6: Order of Battle for Operation Tawakkalna ala Allah 2, June 1988		
Corps	Division	Brigades
Iraq		
Republican Guards Corps	Corps Troops incl. Republican Guards Corps Artillery Brigade	
	Hammurabi Armoured Division Republican Guards	8th & 17th Armoured, 15th Mechanised Brigades Republican Guards Corps
	Medina Manarwah Armoured Division Republican Guards	2nd & 10th Armoured, 14th Mechanised Brigades Republican Guards Corps
	Baghdad Infantry Division Republican Guards	4th, 5th, 6th, 7th Infantry Brigades Republican Guards Corps
	Special Purposes Division Republican Guards	3rd & 16th Special Forces, 26th Naval Commando Brigade Republican Guards Corps
III Corps	Corps Troops, 1st & 2nd Commando Brigades of III Corps; 65th & 66th Special Forces Brigades; III Corps Artillery Brigade	
	1st Mechanised Division	34th Armoured, 1st & 27th Mechanised Brigades
	3rd Armoured Division	6th & 12th Armoured, 8th Mechanised Brigades
	5th Mechanised Division	26th Armoured, 15th & 20th Mechanised Brigades
	6th Armoured Division	16th & 30th Armoured, 25th Mechanised Brigades
	41st Infantry Division	82nd, 105th, 112th Infantry Brigades
	8th Infantry Division (defensive only)	
	19th Infantry Division (defensive only)	
	3rd Wing IrAAC	
	4th Wing IrAAC	
VI Corps	Corps troops; 1st & 2nd Commando Brigades of VI Corps; VI Corps Artillery Brigade	
	25th Infantry Division	87th, 103rd, 428th Infantry, 68th Special Forces Brigades
Iran		
	92nd Armoured Division IRIA	3 brigades
	21st Infantry Division IRIA	3 brigades
	8th Val-Fajr Division IRGC	3 brigades
	12th Qa'em-e Mohammad Mechanised Division IRGC	3 brigades
	14th Imam Hossein Division IRGC	3 brigades
	19th Fajr Infantry Division IRGC	3 brigades; re-deployed during offensive
	30th Beit-ol Moghaddas Armoured Division IRGC	1 mechanised brigade
	64th Suduqu Brigade IRGC	
	84th Zafar Mechanised Brigade IRGC	
	85th Hejrat Mechanised Brigade IRGC	
	163rd Fateme-ye Zahra Brigade IRGC	
	33rd Artillery Group IRIA	
	90th Khatam al-Anbiya Artillery Brigade IRGC	
	91st Hadid Artillery Brigade IRGC	
	2nd Combat Support Group IRIAA	

IrAAC deployed 3rd and 4th Wings and could provide 100 troop-carrying helicopters for Rawi, in addition to gunships. The IrAF provided three strike wings, a bomber squadron, and a squadron of Mirages equipped for photo-reconnaissance and electronic warfare. Meanwhile, as usual by this point in the war, the Iraqis were de-facto free to roam the battlefield almost unchallenged, as Iranian air power reached its nadir.

As petty bickering between Iraqi generals continued, Rawi pressed to strengthen operations on his right and may have hoped to exploit Aboud's 'unselfishness.' On 15 June 1988, the latter withdrew the

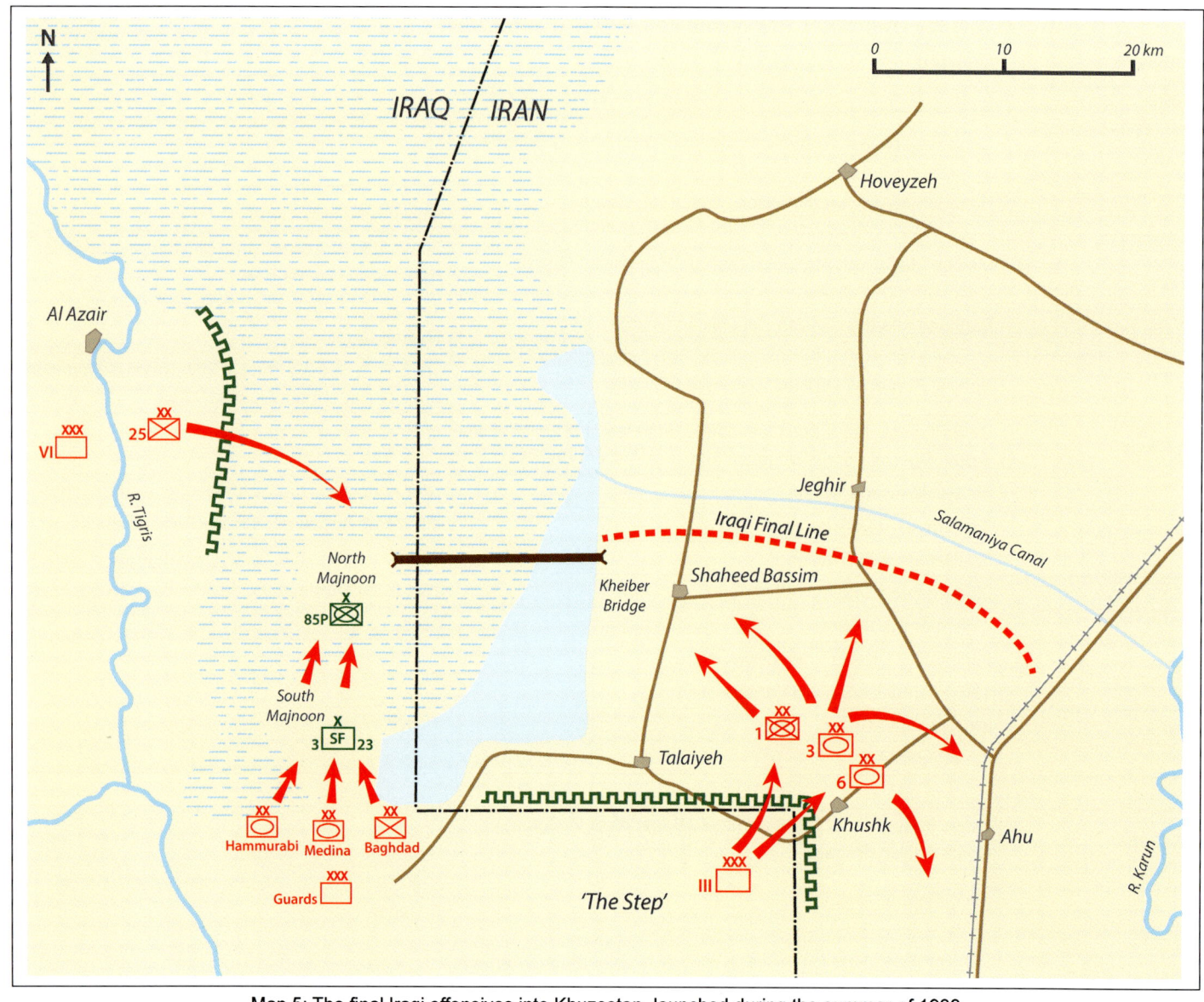

Map 5: The final Iraqi offensives into Khuzestan, launched during the summer of 1988.

assault units from the front for training, and three days later – after Beit-ol-Mogaddas-7 – he attended a AFGC meeting, chaired by Khairallah, still clearly shaken by the Iranian attack. It was suggested, probably by Khazraji, that as insurance against a repeat of Beit al-Moqaddas-7, Aboud should keep one of his mobile divisions on his right flank and that one of Rawi's formations would replace it for the drive across the border. Rawi rightly opposed a scheme which would see his forces advancing on two axes when he wished to advance solely upon South Majnoon. Once again Adoud came to the rescue suggesting he use three rather than four mobile divisions – by leaving 5th Mechanised Division on watch in the south.

He also proposed having another corps headquarters ready to take over 8th and 19th Infantry Divisions, together with 5th Mechanised Division, if the Iranian threat returned. Correspondingly, General Mohammad Abdul Qader's IV Corps was warned it might be deployed for this task.

Thus, Adoud redrafted his plans so the thrust from the bridgehead would now be by the understrength (minus one brigade) armoured division reinforced by an infantry brigade, and push up to 44 North, while the mechanised division (also minus a brigade) would be sent north. This was agreed on 19 June 1988 when Y-Day was set for 25 June with S-Hour at 04:15.

Remnants of the Remnants

Just as the Iraqis had relied upon berm-based defences so did the Iranians who established their FEBA some 2 kilometres inside their own country. Behind the usual wire entanglements and minefields were four hastily-constructed berms, one-behind-the-other to a depth of some 5 kilometres, with high observation towers built into the forward berm to provide early warning of enemy intentions. These poorly-built and shallow defences were manned by two or three tank battalions of 3rd Brigade/92nd IRIA Armoured Division (50 MBT), 2nd Brigade/21st IRIA Infantry and 15 Pasdaran battalions; the battered remnants of divisions which had taken part in the abortive counter-offensive and were still licking their wounds.

The islands, which had similar defences, had been expanded since the failure of Valfajr-8 as part of an extensive Iranian effort to strengthen the southern front. Despite the departure of so many Pasdaran troops, the Iranians had been filling the marshes since the summer of 1987 to double the size of the islands, which now extended to within 5.5 kilometres of the Iraqi positions on the marsh's western bank. They had also extended logistical facilities between Ahvaz and Khorramshahr with numerous camps, supply depots and repair shops and a much-improved road system; activities the CIA interpreted as preparations for a new southern front offensive.[215]

5 END GAME

A medic evacuates an injured soldier from a position of one of few IRIA units deployed on the southern frontlines as seen while under Iraqi artillery fire. (via Tom Cooper)

In too many cases during the final battles on the southern frontlines of the Iran-Iraq War, Iranian defenders were left with little choice but to wait for Iraqi infantry and armour to enter their frontlines before firing back. Here a group of Pasdaran is tensely monitoring the situation in front of their position. (via Tom Cooper)

The Kheiber Bridge still crossed the frontier from the Shaheed Bassim road junction to link North Majnoon with Iran. The island was held by the 85th 'Hejrat' Mechanised Brigade, reinforced by 13 Pasdaran battalions, of which one or two were deployed along the western edge of the marshes. South Majnoon was held by the IRIA's 3rd Brigade/23rd Special Forces Division, reinforced by two Pasdaran battalions and a tank battalion from 92nd Armoured Division, a total of some 8,500 men with 25 MBTs and some guns – of which most of the latter had been withdrawn to the Iranian 'mainland'. The Iranians faced the new threat with no more than 30,000 men with 75 MBTs, supported by 18 artillery battalions now down to 200 guns with limited ammunition. SFOHQ was no doubt anxiously awaiting the arrival of reinforcements from the north, apparently heralded by the deployment around Ahvaz of 19th Fajr Division IRGC with some 6,000 men. It was a forlorn hope, for the Americans observed the Iraqi build-up and, on 18 June, the CIA reported a significant increase in artillery south of the marshes and the deployment of 2,200 AFVs.[216]

Start Basins

During mid-June 1988 there was intense preparatory work behind the Iraqi lines with units again rehearsing assaults on courses specially created to resemble their initial objectives, while amphibious assaults were practised in the Hawr al Hammar, north west of Basra.[217] Much effort was expended to overcome the problems of operating in the marshes and the surrounding boggy ground. Rawi required extra bridging material, together with boats, and had to be helped out by the resources of General Headquarters and the Iraqi Navy, the latter providing 136 seagoing barges and landing craft as well as some hovercraft. Some 48 hours before Y-Day Rawi had assembled 1,680 aluminium and rubber assault boats, some 220 with support weapons.

The problem of launching the Iraqi 'armada' was that the moment boats began assembling along the marsh edge embankments they faced the threat of artillery fire which could inflict heavy losses. A civilian engineer came up with the solution of creating dry docks (the Iraqis called them 'start basins' (Ahwadh al-Intilaq) behind the embankments, in which the boats and the men assembled shortly before S-Hour when holes would be blown in the embankment, filling the dry docks, and allowing the boats to float into the marshes. Rawi's mechanised battalions were stripped to provide a flotilla of 138 BMP-1 amphibious IFVs, augmented by a fleet of 48 GSP amphibious ferries from the Military Engineers' Directorate, while the divisional engineer battalions provided 12 Czech MT-55 AVBLs. The Directorate also provided a 500-metre pontoon bridge which was augmented by Styrofoam floats: 2,700 small ones to form foot-bridges and 830 large ones to support light vehicles.

Aboud concealed his preparations behind a berm built just behind the corps' frontline berm-based defences, where walled laagers were created in the angle of 'The Step' to assemble the armoured units. Engineers also had to prepare routes through III Corps' defences, extend the road network and prepare to bulldoze gaps through the berms. Aboud also had problems with the boggy terrain around the marshes which he would have to traverse to reach Kushk, and this task was assigned to two engineer battalions. They assembled heaps of rock and dry earth which were brought up at night, during which they secretly created along the northern part of 'The Step' 18 12-metre-wide, firm passages through the soft ground at 200-metre intervals up to the enemy FEBA, 5 kilometres inside Iran. In addition, narrower paths were constructed for the infantry and there was more material to create passages beyond the enemy FEBA. To ensure the enemy could not raise the level of water in the marshes, Aboud also arranged with the civil authorities to breach one of the embankments and allow water to drain into the Shatt al-Arab.

While the IrAF and Special Forces probed the marshes to learn all they could of the defences, the planners paid particular attention to deception. This effort was largely carried by VI and III Corps who planned diversions, dummy frontal assaults and amphibious assaults upon the islands, and even encirclement. The first active operations began as soon as the Iranian counter-offensive had been contained and, on 16 June 1988, Rawi's guns began probing the enemy by fire to determine his reactions. Up to 20 batteries, augmented by FROG missiles were delivering 20-minutes barrages at a time. The response was encouragingly weak and when the Guards' batteries repeated their probe the following day there was no reaction as the Iranians decided to conserve their limited ammunition.

What man proposes, God disposes and while there had been some cooling since mid-June with the temperature dropping into the low 40s centigrade, on the afternoon of 24 June, the winds picked up. A very strong North-Westerly wind started to blow causing an easterly surge in the marsh waters which overflowed the southern and eastern banks. Flood waters covered III Corps' three western passages and threatened the fourth. Aboud's prayers were answered by dusk for the winds had died down and the flooding stopped before it reached the fourth passage and thus caused only

An Iraqi mortar crew in action in the dust and heat of the summer 1988. (Albert Grandolini Collection)

A BMP-1 operated by the IRGC, as seen in mid-1988, somewhere on the southern front of the Iran-Iraq War. (Albert Grandolini Collection)

a minor setback. That evening he and Rawi were summoned to 41st Infantry Division headquarters where they met Saddam who passed on his final instructions while final preparations for the offensive were arranged. The temperature the following day was 40° Centigrade, although the wind had increased to 30 km/h rising to 40 km/h when the temperature dropped to 38° Centigrade. On 26 and 27 June 1988, the temperature rose to 44° Centigrade as the wind declined to about 24 km/h.[218]

Operation 'Tawakkalna ala Allah 2'

At 03.45 hours of 25 June 1988, the Iraqis opened their half-hour preparatory bombardment, paying considerable attention to the disruption of Iranian reserves. Even so, the barrage left the waters covered with dead and stunned fish. Unlike the previous offensives, which were launched into largely barren and sparsely populated terrain, Tawakkalna ala Allah 2 had significant impact upon Iraq's post-war economic recovery plans – for the Majnoon oil fields would be a major contributor. For this reason the bombardment relied less upon lethal chemical agents and more upon those which ensured temporary incapacity, such as riot control and CS gas, to prevent the oil field being contaminated. Riot control agents and CS gas came from 82mm and 120mm mortar bombs, while 152mm howitzers fired shells with CS – although more lethal agents were used against the enemy rear network as far north as Hoveyzeh.[219]

Proceeded by air strikes including two squadrons of Tu-22 bombers and two of Su-25 fighter-bombers, the assault went in at 04:15 with the Guards Corps advancing northwards up the land bridge to South Majnoon in three parallel columns, with (west to east) Sattar's Hammurabi, Hammash's Medina, and Shannan's Baghdad Divisions – each led by an infantry brigade supported by three IrAAC squadrons of Bo.105s, Gazelles and Mi-25. T-72 tanks were brought across the marshes on GSP ferries and began providing fire support, while Hanoush's SP Division on the right provided two commando brigades which boarded boats around midnight, floated out of their dry docks without incident when the embankment was blown, and then sailed some three kilometres to land on the island's western bank and attack enemy batteries.

As they landed in the west, the Iraqi second echelon – two infantry brigades in BMPs – began landing on the eastern side. They were delayed by failing engines, and poor navigation aggravated by poor communications. Despite the problems they had pulled the fangs of the defence by the time the third echelon arrived, at S+2, with one armoured brigade brought in by GSP ferries and the other by pontoon bridge. Together, the Guards brigades mopped up to take 1,000 prisoners and a number of MBTs which they turned against their former owners, and by 07:30 the Iraqi flag flew over the island.

The Iraqis then rushed to organise defences and prepare for the next phase of the offensive, as their engineers assembled pontoon bridges to bring in heavy support and also built earth embankments to facilitate the movement of support forces. After two hours, Rawi began assaulting North Majnoon from 09:30 with two of Shannan's infantry brigades, supported by Sattar's and Hammash's mechanised brigades fighting their way across the embankment linking the two islands, landing at 09:40.

Once they established a bridgehead, the second echelon followed with the two commando brigades and an armoured brigade on GSPs, while at 14:40 no less than 57 Mi-17 helicopters landed a commando battalion six kilometres inside Iran – east of the marshes near the Shaheed Bassim junction, to block the Kheiber Bridge's mainland exit. The landing zone came under heavy fire but the Guards suffered light losses and began eliminating those batteries which did not withdraw. The isolated Iranian garrison stubbornly fought on for ten hours as Iraqi engineers built two causeways from South Majnoon to consolidate their grip. Eventually, the island was secured by 19.30. During this final phase, the Guards were assisted by VI Corps which, despite fog, pushed forward with two infantry brigades of the 25th Infantry Division to clear the marshes west of the Majnoons by taking the Iranian-held sandy promontories within the marshes before reaching North Majnoon.

Some of the Majnoon defenders undoubtedly escaped along the myriad of minor paths along embankments but there was no sanctuary for them. Aboud's artillery also began its preparation at 03:45, and 30 minutes later three divisions – from west towards east: 1st Mechanised, 3rd Armoured, and 6th Armoured – advanced from their laagers. The redrafting of plans on 19 June reduced the impact of the loss of passages due to flooding, and by 04:50 the spearheads were on the edge of the enemy defences and requesting a lifting of fire. An infantry brigade and a commando brigade, supported by an armoured brigade, took most of the first three berm lines in just over an hour. The last, some three kilometres away, had fallen after another hour's fighting to establish the bridgehead Aboud was seeking. Now 3rd Armoured Division, reinforced by an infantry

5 END GAME

A still from a video showing a buttoned-down Iraqi Type 69-II advancing in the direction of Iranian positions south of the Majnoons, in June 1988. (Tom Cooper Collection)

A rare photo of a (nearly-intact) Iraqi Bo.105 attack helicopter, as captured by US troops in 2003. The type saw intensive service on the southern frontlines during the last three years of the Iran-Iraq War. (via Pit Weinert)

A HOT ATGM-armed Gazelle of the IrAAC (serial 4237) underway low over forward Iraqi positions. Together with Mi-25s and MD.500s, the type played an important role in providing support for Iraqi offensives in 1988. (Albert Grandolini Collection)

brigade, broke out at 08:00 and pushed north along the Kushk–Jeghir road 'to the east up near the edges of marsh', to envelop the enemy. While Pasdaran formations around it were falling apart, the 92nd Armoured Division desperately resisted in a fighting retreat, aimed at shielding Ahvaz, but lost its commander, Major General Muhammad Ali Shafiee. The Iraqi 1st Mechanised Division (minus its armoured brigade) followed and while 6th Armoured Division masked the Iranian forces around Khorramshahr, it joined 3rd Armoured Division's advance to the ancient Salamaniya Canal, which the Iranians had re-opened and linked to the Karun, then stopped in a landscape of wreckage lit by numerous fires. One of the 1st Division's mechanised brigades took the Shaheed Bassim junction, which was the entrance to the Kheiber Bridge, relieving the Guards commando battalion. In total, the Iraqis had thus taken 800 square kilometres of Iranian territory, together with about 1,000 prisoners and much equipment, before they continued to mop up and push probes northwards to Ahwaz, keeping the enemy off balance.[220]

The advances of Rawi and Aboud were greatly aided by air support. On 25 June 1988, the IrAAC flew 266 gunship sorties while the IrAF flew 247 attack sorties. Their activity continued in similar fashion on the next day, with the IrAAC flying 161 gunship sorties over the battlefield. During mop-up operations of 27 and 28 June, the IrAF still flew 221 combat sorties and the IrAAC another 238. By contrast, the IRIAF managed meagre 35 combat sorties on 25 and 26 June.

Telescoping the Conclusion

The collapse of Iranian resistance meant Aboud was able to telescope the second and third phases: within two hours his men were between Jeghir and Kushk rounding up as many prisoners as they could, 1st Mechanised Division receiving an infantry battalion to help them in this task. This division reached Shaheed Bassim at midday, while 3rd Armoured Division went onto Jeghir some 20 kilometres across the border. Then, in response to a query from Saddam, who was visiting III Corps forward command post, Aboud sent a brigade of 3rd Armoured Division to Ahu rail station to cut the Ahvaz-Khorramshahr highway and rail line and destroy as much stored material as possible. The division also pushed ahead to the Salamaniya Canal to seize and demolish two bridges which crossed it. A trench-digging machine was brought forward in the early afternoon and used to break embankments leading from Iran to North Majnoon, while observation towers in the captured enemy defences were demolished. Meanwhile, 3rd Armoured Division spent the afternoon emptying or destroying enemy supply dumps. Finally, at 18.00hrs, Aboud gave the order for a general withdrawal across the border.

This final action, made to demonstrate the Iraqi acceptance of the modified UN Resolution 598 – which was to be the basis of a ceasefire – still provided sufficient opportunity for transfer of the booty to Iraq. Namely, the Iraqis actually remained on Iranian territory for the entire 26 June, and withdrew only when the last piece of captured equipment and the last prisoner of war had been sent across the border. In their wake, they left carefully laid minefields and then plugged the gaps in their defensive berms. Indeed, during the General Army Command meeting on 27 June, Aboud was criticised for not bringing back more prisoners due to slipshod searching for scattered Iranian troops.[221]

The Iraqis claimed, probably accurately, that their offensive had mauled between six and eight Iranian divisions, resulted in the capture of 5,000 prisoners (nearly 1,650 by Aboud), 57 MBTs, 24 AFVs and large quantities of weapons, while inflicting up to 9,000 casualties. In return, by 27 June 1988, the Iraqis should had suffered 368 killed (including 69 dead of the Guards Corps) and about 900 wounded. However, there were reports in which the 25th Division might have also suffered heavy casualties.[222]

Immense Booty

There was no Iranian reaction to the Iraqi offensive into the Hawizeh Marshes. Instead, Tehran bitterly complained about the extensive use of chemical weapons by Iraq – which eventually proved to be one of the major reasons for increasing numbers of young Iranians becoming reluctant to volunteer for military service. Having denied the use of such weapons for years, on 1 July 1988 the Iraqi Foreign Minister Tariq Aziz publicly admitted it, but added a claim that the Iranians used chemical weapons on many occasions, too. Responding to Western criticism, Aziz added 'There are different views on this matter from different angles. You are living on a civilised continent. You are living on a peaceful continent.'[223]

Overall, since March 1988, the Iraqis had claimed the capture of 1,298 MBTs, 155 IFVs, 512 guns, 6,196 mortars, 5,550 light guns and pieces of recoilless artillery, 60,694 rifles, 454 trucks and 1,600 light vehicles and trailers – in essence nearly all of the heavy weapons of the Iranian ground forces. In comparison, about 570 MBTs, 130 BMP-1s and Scorpions, 300 APCs, 320 towed- and 45 self-propelled guns, and 300 anti-aircraft guns were put on display in Baghdad in July the same year – and, certainly enough, many of these had been captured early during the war. Nevertheless, related publications resulted in reports about complete exhaustion of the regular Iranian military, and de-facto the demise of the IRIAF. Similarly, Iranian oppositionals in Iraq estimated that Iran would require US$15-20 billion spent over five years to rebuild its forces.[224]

The Nail in the Coffin: Tawakkalna ala Allah-4

With the conclusion of 'Tawakkalna ala Allah 2' the southern front now became a backwater, although one in which the Iranians were constantly on the alert for new thrusts towards Ahvaz or Abadan. The central front, reinforced by Rawi's corps, now became the focus of Iraqi efforts; beginning at Mehran with Operation 'Tawakkalna ala Allah-3 from 12 July, followed from 22 July 1988 by Operation Tawakkalna ala Allah-4. The latter became one of the biggest ever Iraqi offensives on this part of the frontline.

Together these operations not only inflicted heavy blows upon the Iranians, but forced them to disperse their forces and delayed the passage of large troop contingents from north towards the south. A crumb of comfort for Tehran was the destruction of a major incursion by the Iraqi-backed Iranian emigrés of the Mujahideen e-Khalq (MEK, also MKO) or National Liberation Army (NLA).[225]

Tawakkalna ala Allah-4 provided Aboud's III Corps with one last 'hurrah'. Although minor in comparison to the three earlier operations with this title, it allowed him to complete the disruption of the enemy infra-structure in the south. On 23 July 1988, the 3rd and 6th Armoured, 1st Mechanised, 8th, 11th, 19th and 30th Infantry Divisions crossed the border to carve out a 25-kilometre wide and 65-kilometre-deep bridgehead, only 25 kilometres southwest of the provincial capital Ahvaz. The operation was led by Brigadier-General Tahir's 3rd Armoured Division, which overran the major Iranian camp around Hamid during the night. Tahir was killed in a helicopter crash, but this remained the only set-back for Iraqis, and thus they were left free to plunder and then destroy the enemy logistics depots before withdrawing unhindered across the border.[226]

The Last Hurrah

The elections of April 1988 in Iran had reflected Khomeini's growing public antipathy to conservative traditionalists, and resulted in a Majlis dominated by more liberal representatives. Amid growing tensions between the hawks and new parliamentaries – clashes between them were prevented only by Khoemini's intervention, on 24 May – the Iraqi attacks into Iran prompted large number of Iranians to follow renewed calls on arms. Even the Majlis closed to allow its members to go fighting, while thousands of civil servants,

An Iraqi Type-69-II in hull-down position near the Iranian border, summer 1988. (via Pit Weinert)

clerics, and students left for the front: they all arrived much too late.

Furthermore, there were more pressing economic reasons for ending the war. Already in March 1988, the Budget and Planning Ministry warned that in the light of dwindling revenues the current rate of military expenditure could be maintained only with a 25 per cent cut in social expenditure. Rafsanjani's promotion in the aftermath of Tawakkalna ala Allah-1 saw the Iranian Foreign Ministry intensify its efforts to seek a diplomatic solution. The United Nations had proposed a cease-fire agreement as Resolution 598 – which Iran accepted in February 1988 – but Tehran mistrusted the international organisation. It was Khomeini, who sought to neutralize the IRGC's influence and opposition to its acceptance through appointing Rafsanjani as Commander-in-Chief – who saw this as the basis for ending the war.[227]

On 30 June 1988, the same day Mir Hussein Musavi was appointed the Prime Minister, that Tehran officially conceded that it had suffered major military reverses – which it blamed on the Superpowers' 'unholy alliance'. On 3 July the American cruiser USS *Vincennes* shot down, in error, an Iranian airliner with the loss of 290 lives. Tehran requested an emergency meeting of the UN Security Council.

The UN body was that month chaired by West Germany, one of the few European countries which had provided 'soft-skinned' vehicles – but no arms – to the combatants, and its relative neutrality made it acceptable to Tehran. Resolution 598 was redrafted to include the establishment of a commission of inquiry into the war's origins and was generally accepted on 20 July 1988. A few days later German Foreign Minister Hans Dietrich Genscher publicly rebuked Iraq both for starting the war and for using chemical weapons and – by establishing his credentials as an independent – he cemented Germany's position with Iran. Baghdad was less welcoming, but Saddam – who now had military superiority – was willing to accept a diplomatic solution knowing he had leverage through the equivalent of a $2 billion debt to Bonn.

On 14 July 1988 Iran's leaders met and agreed to accept Resolution 598, the cabinet ratifying this decision the next day in a meeting attended by Rafsanjani, while on 16 July Khomeini wrote to express his agreement. This decision was passed to the UN within 24 hours and Khomeini formally announced it to the nation on 20 July, adding that accepting it: "...was more deadly for me than taking poison. I submit myself to God's will and drank this drink for His satisfaction."

The decision astonished the world. Indeed, on 17 August the

Between Iranian artillery pieces captured by the Iraqis towards the end of the war, are also this 35mm Oerlikon GDF-001 anti-aircraft gun (centre) and 155mm M1/M59 'Long Tom' field howitzer (right side). (Albert Grandolini Collection)

Jubilant Iraqi Army troops cheering the cease-fire that ended eight years of war with Iran, in August 1988. (via Ali Tobchi)

CIA had to write a report explaining its failure to predict it. It admitted its analysts had failed to anticipate it but, in an example of bureaucratic face-saving, claimed a minority of them had recognized Iran's growing interest in diplomacy and the amount of support for Rafsanjani.[228]

Saddam was more reluctant to accept the ceasefire, for he believed the enemy were only playing for time. Furthermore, he was determined to achieve his pre-war aims of gaining territory and controlling the Shatt al-Arab. Yet by late July it was obvious there was a strategic impasse and the two sides quickly began to hammer out a UN sponsored cease-fire. A corresponding agreement was reached on 8 August to take effect at 03:00 on 20 August 1988 with a UN military observer group as the controlling body.

While many of post-war estimates put the war dead at 300,000 or more (sometimes to over 1 million), and while no official figures were ever made available for Iraqi casualties, on 18 September 1988, Islamic Guidance Minister Mohammed Khatami said the country had lost 123,220 combatants and 11,000 civilians killed. The army lost 35,170 dead and the Pasdaran 79,664.[229]

After eight years of bloody conflict the war ended virtually where it had begun. There would be no diplomatic agreement between Baghdad and Tehran until 1990, when Saddam sought to recoup his diplomatic and economic loses with the disastrous invasion of Kuwait. This delayed a full repatriation of prisoners until 1993. Meanwhile, in 1991, the Iraqi military was taught a sharp lesson in modern military sciences by a collection of US and European armies which had been preparing for a high-intensity conflict for 40 years.

Chapter 5 notes

212 For details on the Hawizah Marshes see Volume 2 pp.19-20
213 For 'Tawakkalna ala Allah 2' see Cooper & Bishop p.276; Farrokh pp.410-411; Hiro p209-210, 238; Khazraji pp. 537-560; Lessons pp. 388-390, 408 f/n 81;Makki pp 331-332, 335-345, 348-376; Marashi and Salama p.172; Malovany pp. 433-440; Murray & Woods pp. 327-332; Pelletiere p.144; Pollack pp.227-228; Ward pp.293-294; Iraqi Offensive in Majnoon Island Area Begins at gulflink.osd.mil/declassified/cia/19961102/110296_93663-72538_01.text; CIA National Intelligence Dailies at foia.cia.gov/browse_docs.asp 18 and 22 June, and Iran- Iraq Frontline entry in web site gulflink.osd.mil.
214 Iraqi strengths based upon the order-of-battle and DIA DDB-2680-103-88 p.14.
215 CIA-RDP90T00114R000700800002-2
216 Shaheed Bassim had distinguished himself in the marsh battles in which he was killed. CIA National Intelligence Dailies June 18. Murray & Woods p.327 identify the Majnoon defenders as '85th Pasdaran Brigade and the 3rd Armoured Brigade of the 23rd Pasdaran Division.' In fact the 85th 'Hejrat' Pasdaran Brigade was a mechanised unit usually of two infantry and one tank battalions but the armoured unit had been reduced to a company of 10 MBT. The 23rd Division was the IRIA Special Forces formation and would not have had an armoured formation, especially in that terrain.
217 There was no time left to train attacks on the secondary objectives.
218 Meteorological data from nearby Kuwait on Freemeteo web site
219 Ironically, the CIA noted, 'No evidence of chemical weapons use was in the battle areas. The two decontamination stations had not moved and there was no discernible activity'. CIA National Intelligence Dailies 26-27 June 1988 & CIA National Intelligence Daily 27 June 1988
220 The CIA reported that the Iraqis stopped at 31-11N 48-10E and 31-09N 47-55E
221 CRRC SH-SHTP-D-000-538
222 The Iraqi figure probably includes both elements of divisions and independent brigades. CRRC SH-SHTP-D-000-538.
223 Lessons p. 389
224 Lessons pp. 395-6; Atkeson, *Iraq's Arsenal: Tool of Ambition*; & 'Iran needs '$15-25b to rebuild forces', *Jane's Defence Weekly*, 4 February 1989.
225 These events will be described in Volume 4.
226 He was the brother of the VII Corps commander General Maher Abd al-Rashid. Our thanks to General Makki for this information.
227 For the background to the war's end see Bulloch & Morris pp. 237-238, 245, 248-249; Hiro pp. 206, 210-211, 232-233, 241-249; Razoux pp.455-468.
228 CIA-RDP90G01353R001200090002-2 17 August 1988
229 JDW Revolutionary Guards.

CAMOUFLAGE AND MARKINGS

Photographs of Iraqi T-72s from the period 1987-1988 are extremely rare. Those of surviving examples from the original batch of 125 tanks delivered in 1980 – even more so. This example was last seen in summer 1988, meanwhile mostly re-painted in yellow sand, with only minimal touches of blue-green. (Artwork by Tom Cooper)

This almost brand-new T-72M was captured by the Iranians sometimes in 1987. Most of the vehicle was painted in green overall, but front parts of the turret and most of the gun were camouflaged with mud, or grey sand colour. The vehicle only received a turret number (113) before it was sent to the frontlines. (Artwork by Tom Cooper)

By 1988, most of the vehicles assigned to units of the Republican Guards Corps were painted in yellow sand overall. Polish-supplied T-72Ms were originally painted in a "cardboard" colour, but this rapidly faded in the sun and sand. They received various identification insignia, including front and rear ends of fenders trimmed in white, and about 60-centimetre long 'ID-stripes' in white, green or black on their skirts. Some T-72Ms received the inscription 'Assad Babil' (Lion of Babylon) instead. Insets show (left upper corner) complex tactical insignia used by the Medinah Manarwah Armoured Division, Tawakkalna ala Allah Armoured Division, and Nebuchadnezar Infantry Division respectively. If applied, these were placed on the rear of the turret-stowage box, together with individual identification – or the 'turret number' of the tank in question, and the letter 'J' (short of 'Jaysh', Army). (Artwork by Tom Cooper)

CAMOUFLAGE AND MARKINGS

The majority of other heavy vehicles of the Iraqi Army were re-painted in yellow sand overall by 1988. This T-55 had its fume extractor painted in yellow, with a white strip: this was one of most widespread methods of identification for Iraqi tanks in this war. Furthermore, it had its tactical unit insignia applied on the turret. Sadly, the background of the latter remains unknown. (Artwork by Tom Cooper)

Probably belonging to the same mechanised battalion of an unknown Iraqi brigade – and captured by the IRGC on the same occasion as the T-55 shown in the previous profile – was this BMP-1. Painted yellow sand overall, it also wore its unit's tactical insignia: the red and white square was applied near the centre of the vehicle, instead of further towards the front, as more usual. Insets show various other tactical unit insignia of various Iraqi brigades. Sadly, no backgrounds of these are currently known. (Artwork by Tom Cooper)

This BMP-1 was captured by the IRGC during Operation Karbala-5 and instantly pressed into service against its former owners. Uncharacteristically for 1987, it was still camouflaged in yellow sand and blue-green, indicating it might have been in service with the Iraqi Army since the early 1980s. It is possible that this BMP-1 received the large turret number '21' – applied in white or yellow – too. (Artwork by Tom Cooper)

By 1988, the Iraqi Army had received its first batches of BMP-2s, and these saw some service during final stages of the war with Iran. As far as is known, all of these were painted in the same fashion as the Polish-made T-72Ms. This example would have been assigned to one of the brigades of the 3rd Armoured Division, tactical insignia of which was applied on the side of the front hull. The meaning of the yellow 'bar' directly above it remains unknown. (Artwork by Tom Cooper)

Another new appearance in the Iraqi Army of the late 1980s were Chinese-made YW-531 APCs. Apparently operated by mechanised brigades of infantry divisions only, all seem to have been painted in dark sand colour overall, and most received their parent-unit's tactical insignia applied on the forward hull. (Artwork by Tom Cooper)

This BMP-1 seems to have survived in service with the IRGC for long enough to receive at least three different sets of inscriptions over time. Except for 'Onion' (stylized word 'Allah'), applied in white atop the gunner's hatch on the turret and in light blue on the front of the fuselage, these included various citations from the Qoran, applied in black and red along the hull. (Artwork by Tom Cooper)

CAMOUFLAGE AND MARKINGS

Indicative of significant problems with identification friend or foe on the battlefields of the Iran-Iraq War, where both sides used vehicles of the same or similar design, this T-55 operated by the IRGC received large ID-markings. Except for Iranian national colours applied around the smoke extractor, it had a big national flag of the Islamic Republic of Iran applied over most of its rear turret. Inscribed on the turret's side was another citation from the Qoran. Otherwise, this T-55 seems to have retained its original coat of olive green (probably applied well before it was captured from the Iraqis), over which wide stripes in mint-green were applied to enhance its camouflage. (Artwork by Tom Cooper)

North Korean-made, and Iranian-operated, 170mmm self-propelled M1979 Koksan guns became notorious during Iranian offensives on Basra, in 1987 when they randomly shelled the city. Firing rocket-assisted projectiles, they could shell targets out to 60 kilometres away – which made them the world's longest-range field artillery pieces in service. Operated by the IRGC only, they retained their original colour of olive green with a strong bluish touch – and even Red Stars made of iron – while wearing no other ID-insignia at all. (Artwork by Peter Penev)

Manufactured by the Second Machine Industry, and installed on a Chinese Type-59 tank chassis, the Koksan guns were only exported to Iran. However, a few IRGC-operated M1979s were captured by Iraq during the campaigns of 1988, and re-painted as shown here. It remains unclear if any of these saw combat service by the end of the Iran-Iraq War. (Artwork by Peter Penev)

A reconstruction of the Iraqi Mi-25 ('Hind') helicopter gunship. Its serial number – 2148 – confirms the delivery of a third – previously unknown – batch of this type to Iraq during the 1980s. Their camouflage colours included yellow sand and green on upper surfaces and sides and were applied in the same pattern as examples exported to a number of other customers (amongst others: Afghanistan, Libya, and Nicaragua). Notable is that the large national flag applied on the front of the cabin of this second batch of Iraqi Mi-25s was slightly narrower than that applied on the first batch. (Artwork by Tom Cooper)

While exported by the USA to Iraq 'for agricultural purposes', 30 Hughes (later McDonnell Douglas Helicopter Systems) MD.500D helicopters were all taken up by the Iraqi Army Aviation Corps and saw intensive combat service during the last three years of the war with Iran. As far as is known, most were painted in yellow sand overall, although some did receive a more complex, three-colour camouflage pattern reminiscent of that applied on many of Iraqi Mi-17s. Armament confirmed as deployed by IrAAC's MD.500Ds included FN ENTA TMP-5 pods for twin 7.62mm machine guns (shown here), but also 12-tube FZ launchers for unguided 2.75in rockets and Brandt 22x68 launchers (for 22 68mm unguided rockets). (Artwork by Tom Cooper)

Iraq acquired a total of no less than 75 Bo.105Ds, and at least four Bo.105Cs, manufactured by Messerschmitt-Bölkow-Böhm in former West Germany, and at least 24 CASA-made Bo.105Ps. A few of these served for SAR purposes, while a handful was equipped as VIP-transports, but most of the Bo.105Ds served with the IrAAC as scout- and attack-helicopters. A few received a calibre 20mm, Swiss-made Oerlikon KAA cannon installed under the cabin, but their primary armament armament consisted of HOT ATGMs, and various pods for unguided rockets (such as Brandt 22x68s). (Artwork by Tom Cooper)

BIBLIOGRAPHY

Books

Buchan, James, *Days of God: The revolution in Iran and its consequences* (London: John Murray, 2013).

Bulloch, John and Harvey Morris, *The Gulf War: Origin, History and Consequences of Islam at War* (London: Methuen Publishers, 1989).

Cooper, Tom & Farzad Bishop, *Iran-Iraq War in the Air 1980-1988* (Atglen: Schiffer Military History, 2000).

Cooper, Tom & Babak Taghvaee and Liam F. Devlin, *IRIAF 2010* (Houston: Harpia Publishing, 2010).

Cordesman, Anthony H., *The Iran-Iraq War and Western Security 1984-1987* (RUSI Military Power Series), (London: Jane's Publishing Company Ltd, 1987).

Cordsman, Anthony H. & Abraham R. Wagner, *The Lessons of Modern War: Volume II-The Iran-Iraq War* (Boulder/San Francisco Westview Press and London: Mansell Publishing Ltd,1990).

Farrokh, Dr Kaveh, *Iran at War 1500-1980* (Botley: Osprey Publishing, 2011).

Foss, Christopher (editor), *Jane's Armour and Artillery, 1996-1997* (Coulsdon: Jane's Information Group, 1996).

Foss, Christopher (editor),*Jane's Armour and Artillery, 2007-2008* (Coulsdon: Jane's Information Group, 2007).

Hiro, Dilip, *The Longest War: The Iran-Iraq Military Conflict* (London: Paladin Grafton Books, 1989).

Khazraji, General (General Staff) Nizar Abdul Karim Faisal Al, *Al Harb Al Iraqiya- Al Iraniya) 1980-1988 Muthakerat Muqatel (The Iraq-Iran War1980-1988. Memoirs of a Fighter)* (Doha, Qatar: Arab Centre for Research & Policy Studies, 2014).

Khoury, Dina Rizk, *Iraq in Wartime: Soldiering, Martyrdom and Remembrance* (Cambridge: Cambridge University Press, 2013).

Makki Khamas (Makki) General Aladdin Hussein, *Maarik Al Tahrir Al Kubra Al Iraqiya 1988 (The Great Iraqi Battles of Liberation 1988)*(Amman, Jordan: Academiuoon Publishing Company, 2014).

Malovany, Colonel Pesach, *Milhamot Bavel ha-Hadasha (The Wars of Modern Babylon)*(Tel Aviv: Ma'arachot, 2010).

Al-Marashi, Ibrahim & Sammy Salama, *Iraq's Armed Forces: An analytical history* (London: Routledge, 2009).

Murray, Williamson and Kevin M. Woods, *The Iran-Iraq War: A Military and Strategic History* (Cambridge: Cambridge University Press, 2014).

National Training Center, *The Iraqi Army: organization and tactics* (Boulder: Colorado Paladin Press, 1991).

Nejad, Parviz Mosalla (Editor), *Shalamcheh* (Shalamcheh: Sarir Publication, 2006). Downloaded from web site Shalamcheh Author: The Hub of Resistance Litterature &History (http)sajed.ir/upload%5Ctopic%5Cebook-Shalamcheh.pdf.

O'Ballance, Edgar, *The Gulf War,* (London: Brassey's Defence Publishers, 1988).

Pelletiere, Stephen C., *The Iran-Iraq War: Chaos in a Vacuum* (Westport CT and London: Praeger, 1992).

Pollack, Kenneth M., *Arabs at War. Military effectiveness 1948-1991* (Lincoln, Neb & London: University of Nebraska Press, 2002).

Pollack, Kenneth M., *The Persian Puzzle* (New York: Random House, 2004).

Razoux, Pierre (translated by Nicholas Elliott), *The Iran-Iraq War* (London: The Belnap Press of Harvard University Press, 2015).

Brig.Gen. Ahmad Sadik & Tom Cooper, *Iraqi Fighters, 1953-2003: Camouflage & Markings* (Houston: Harpia Publishing, 2008).

Scales, Brigadier General Robert H. (Director Desert Storm Study Project), *Certain Victory: The United States Army in the Gulf War* (Washington DC: Office of the Chief-of-Staff, United States Army, 1993).

Ward, Steven R., *Immortal: A military history of Iran and its armed forces* (Washington DC: Georgetown University Press, 2009).

Woods, Kevin M. (With Williamson Murray & Thomas Holaday with Mounir Elkhamri), *Project 1946* (Alexandria: Virginia Institute for Defense Analyses, 2008).

Woods, Kevin M., (With Murray Williamson, Elizabeth A. Nathan, Laila Sabara, Ana M.Veneger) *Saddam's Generals: Perspectives of the Iran-Iraq War* (Alexandria: Institute for Defense Analysis, 2010).

Woods, Kevin M., *The Mother of all Battles: Saddam Hussein's strategic plan for the Persian Gulf War* (Annapolis: US Naval Institute Press, 2008).

Zabih, Sepehr, *The Iranian military in Revolution and War* (London: Routledge, 1988 and Abindon,Routledge, 2011).

Articles, Essays, Monographs, Papers, Reports, Theses

Aldridge, Colonel B., British Defence Attaché, Baghdad, A Review of the Military Situation in Iraq Over the Period April 1986 to April 1987 (21 May, 1987). Kindly provided by the Foreign Office under the Freedom of Information Act.

Ali, Javed, 'Chemical Weapons and the Iran-Iraq War: A Case Study in Noncompliance', *The Nonproliferation Review* (Spring 2001).

Boyne, Sean, 'Saddam's shield: The role of the Special Republican Guard', *Jane's Intelligence Review* (January 1999) pp 29-32.

Bruce, James, 'No sign of counter-attack by Iraqis', *Jane's Defence Weekly* (21 February 1987), p.265.

Childs, Nick, 'The Gulf War: Iraq under pressure' *Jane's Defence Weekly* (9 May 1987) pp.899-901.

Davis, Major Mark J., 'Iranians' Operational Warfighting Ability: An Historical Assessment and View to the Future', *School of Advanced Military Studies*, United States Army and Command General Staff College, Fort Leavenworth, Kansas (1992).

Eshel, Lieutenant Colonel David, 'Fighting Under Desert Conditions', *Armor* Vol 99 No 6, (November-December 1990).

Forouzan, Adar, 'Iranian Tank Commander', *Military History* (Herndon, VA.) Apr 2004. Vol. 21, Issue 1 pp. 44-46 (In Iran-heritage.org/interestgroups/war-iraqiran-news2.htm).

Griffin, Lieutenant Colonel Gary B., 'The Iraqi Way of War: An operational assessment', *School of Advanced Military Studies,*United States Army Command and General Staff College, Fort Leavenworth, Kansas (1990).

Heyman, Charles, 'Advance of the Intelligent Battlefield: The current world market for anti-personnel mines', *Jane's Defence Weekly* (1997).

Jupa, Richard and James Dingeman, 'The Republican Guards: Loyal, Aggressive, Able', *Army*, (March 1991) pp.54-62.

No author, 'How Saddam kept deadly gas secret', *Independent* (3 July 1998).

No author, 'Growing indications of another Basra offensive', *Jane's Defence Weekly* (10 October 1987).

No author, 'Iran's assault in Iraq-A morale booster? *Jane's Defence Weekly* (25 June 1988).

No author, 'Iran masses troops for major offensive in Gulf', *Jane's Defence Weekly* (28 November 1987).

No author, 'Iran's men of influence', *Jane's Defence Weekly* (30 June 1990).

No author, 'Iran needs '$15-25b to rebuild forces', claim, *Jane's Defence Weekly*, (4 February 1989.).

No author, 'Iran tries to remould revolutionary guards', *Jane's Defence Weekly*, (1 October 1988).

No author, 'The international arms industry: Final casualty of the Gulf War', *Jane's Defence Weekly* (30 July 1988).

No author, 'Mobilisation problem for Iranian leaders', *Jane's Defence Weekly* (2 April 1988).

O'Ballance, Colonel Edgar, 'Iran vs Iraq: Quantity vs Quality?' *Defence Attaché* (No 1/1987) pp.25-31.

Philipps, Richard, 'Tactical Defensive Doctrine of the Iraqi Ground Forces', *Jane's Soviet Intelligence Review* (March 1991) pp.116-119.

Warford, Captain James M., 'The Tanks Of Babylon Main Battle Tanks Of The Iraqi Army', *Armor*, Vol 99 No 6 (November-December 1990).

Documents

CIA

CIA-DOC_ 0000072254.pdf: Iraq's Chemical Warfare Program: More Self-Reliant, More Deadly August 1990.

CIA-DOC_00010797.pdf: Impact and Implications of Chemical Weapons Use in the Iran-Iraq War 20 March 1988.

CIA-RDP86T01017R000808180001-5: The Iran-Iraq War; Impact of the Wet Season. 2 December 1986.

CIA-RDP86T01017R000202020001-4: After Al Faw: Implications and Options for Iraq and Iran 12 March 1986.

CIA-RDP86T01017R000302670001-2: Iran's Improving Ground Forces. 10 July 1986.

CIA-RDP86T01017R00050539001-8: Soviet Military Forces Opposite Iran and In Afghanistan 18 November 1986.
CIA-RDP89S01450R000200230001-0: Iran's Ground Forces: Morale and Manpower Problems. April 1988.
CIA-RDP89S01450R000600600001-5: Iran-Iraq: A Comparison of Two War-Weary economies. November 1988.
CIA-RDP90G01353R001200090002-2: An Evaluation of DI Reporting on Iran's Acceptance of a Cease-Fire in the Iran-Iraq War 17 August 1988.
CIA-RDP90R00961R000300060001-1: Is Iraq Losing the War? April 1986.
CIA-RDP90T00114R000700800002-2: Iran's Preparations for the Next Offensive 15 December 1987.
CIA-RDP90T01298R000300670001-8: The Iraqi Chemical Weapons Program in Perspective 1985.
Conflict Record Research Center (CRRC)
SH-ADGC-D-000-731: Transcript from three Audio Files of a Meeting of the General Command of the Armed Forces March 24 1988.
SH-AFGC-D-000-686: Orders of the President and Commander-in-Chief of the Armed Forces February-December 1984.
SH-GMID-D-000-266: General Military Intelligence Directorate Correspondence about Iranian Military Sites and Plans during the Iraq-Iran War 1987-1988.
SH-GMID-D-000-301 Reports from General Directorate of Military Intelligence regarding the Iraq and Iran War 1982-1987.
SH-GMID-D-000-302: Iran-Iraq Military Activity Report 1981.
SH-GMID-D-000-529: Comprehensive Study of Al-Khomeini Guards during the Iranian-Iraqi War in 1988. October 1988.
SH-GMID-D-001-369: Correspondence between the GMID, the Ministry of Defence, and the Ministry of Interior regarding Iranian military movements and the distribution of Iranian troops, 1985.
SH-IDGS-D-000-854: Reports by the General Security Intelligence Directorate to the Deputy Directorate regarding a study presented by the American Military Attache in Baghdad detailing Iranian military capabilities and Iranian anti-armour weapons purchases. Dec-86 to Mar-88.
SH-PDWN-D-000-730: Transcript of an Armed Forces General Command meeting regarding the Iran-Iraq War, al-Fao, and military and diplomatic aspects of the war. May 26, 1988.
SH-SHTP-D-000-538: Transcript of a Meeting between Saddam and his Commanding Officers at the Armed Forces General Command Regarding the Iraq-Iran War. June 27 1988.
SH-SPPC-D-000-229 Handwritten letter from Saddam Hussein to the Chief-of-Staff advising him in war issues. June 5 1988.

Defense Intelligence Agency
DDB-1100-342-86: Ground Forces Intelligence Study-Iran (May 1986).
DDB-1100-343-85: Ground Forces Intelligence Study: Iraq (November 1985).
DDB-2680-103-88 Part II: Military Intelligence Summary: Volume III, Part II
Middle East and North Africa (Persian Gulf) (Cut-off date 1 July 1987).
US Army Intelligence and Security Command
Untitled and undated history of Iran-Iraq War from September 1980 to the spring of 1983.
Released under NGIA FOIA request NGA #20130255F and US Army Intelligence and Security Command request FOIA#2456F-12 on November 19, 2013. Declassified March 19, 2013.
Foreign Broadcast Interception Service (FBIS)
FBIS-NES-93-074 Saddam Address on al-Faw Anniversary (April 19, 1993)

Websites
AllRefer Country Study and Country guide, Iran. (http) (allrefer.com/country-guide-study/iran/iran155.html). Iran- The Revolutionary Period and Supreme defence Council of Iran
AllRefer.com, Country Study and Country guide (allrefer.com/country-guide-study), Iran (http) (allrefer.com/country-guide-study/iran/iran155.html)
CIA FOIA (https) cia.gov/library/reading room/home
Cipher Machines web site (http) ciphermachines.com
CIA National Intelligence Dailies from web sites (www.) foia.cia.gov/browse_docs.asp
Iraqi Offensive in Majnoon Island Area Begins
Freemeteo web site
(http) Freemeteo.com. Weather History, Kuwait and Diyarkabir. Daily archive
(www) harvardmun.org/wp-content/uploads/2012/01/JCCIran1.pdf.
(http) iiarmy.topcities.com/army/ground/iigf.html. February 6, 2003
Imposed War web site (www) sarjed.ir or (http) English.tebyan,net.
(www) Ironsides8m.com/army/ir.htm~army
Iraqi Armed Forces Forum web site (www: http) Iraqmilitary.org
Kuwait web site
kuwait pages:kuwait wars (http): kuwaitpages.blogspot. com/2007/08/kuwait-wars.html.
Web site (www) gulflink.osd.mil/declassified/cia/19961102/110296_93663-72538_01.text